CAMBRIDGE LIBRARY COLLECTION

Books of enduring scholarly value

Religion

For centuries, scripture and theology were the focus of prodigious amounts of scholarship and publishing, dominated in the English-speaking world by the work of Protestant Christians. Enlightenment philosophy and science, anthropology, ethnology and the colonial experience all brought new perspectives, lively debates and heated controversies to the study of religion and its role in the world, many of which continue to this day. This series explores the editing and interpretation of religious texts, the history of religious ideas and institutions, and not least the encounter between religion and science.

China's Spiritual Need and Claims

James Hudson Taylor (1832–1905), the founder of the large and respected China Inland Mission, wrote the pamphlet *China's Spiritual Need and Claims* in 1865. It was subsequently published as a book and reprinted in numerous editions. This volume contains the seventh edition, first published in 1887. The work is both a survey of Protestant missionary activity in China since the treaty of Tientsin in 1858 and a recruitment pamphlet that inspired many English men and women to travel to China as missionaries. It provides a wealth of demographic and cultural information about nineteenth-century China and about the western missionaries stationed there. As one of the most popular works on Protestant missions during the nineteenth century, it is an essential source for understanding the motivations of Victorian missionaries in general as well as Taylor's own beliefs. It is an indispensable source for researchers in mission history.

China's Spiritual Need and Claims

James Hudson Taylor

CAMBRIDGE UNIVERSITY PRESS

Cambridge, New York, Melbourne, Madrid, Cape Town, Singapore,
São Paolo, Delhi, Dubai, Tokyo

Published in the United States of America by Cambridge University Press, New York

www.cambridge.org
Information on this title: www.cambridge.org/9781108014519

This edition first published 1887
This digitally printed version 2010

ISBN 978-1-108-01451-9 Paperback

CHINA'S SPIRITUAL NEED AND CLAIMS.

BY

J. HUDSON TAYLOR, M.R.C.S., F.R.G.S

OF THE CHINA INLAND MISSION.

SEVENTH EDITION.

LONDON:

MORGAN & SCOTT, 12, PATERNOSTER BUILDINGS, E.C.

1887.

PREFATORY NOTE TO THE SEVENTH EDITION.

IN the year 1865 I was led to write the pamphlet "*China's Spiritual Need and Claims*," shewing the urgent necessity there was for some further effort for the evangelization of China. Its circulation was blessed by GOD, and much interest in China was awakened. A number of persons were led to devote themselves to Mission work there; some who joined the CHINA INLAND MISSION, and some who are members of other Missions, point to that book as having determined their course.

A second edition was published in 1866; a third in 1868; and a fourth in 1872; but for a number of years it was out of print, and friends often urged its re-issue. A revised and enlarged edition, with many illustrations and diagrams, was published in June, 1884. It was hoped that in its improved form it might be more widely blessed than before, in promoting interest in Missionary work in China. That fifth edition of 5000 copies being exhausted, a sixth edition, also of 5000 copies, substantially the same, only a few typographical corrections having been inserted, was issued the same year. The present edition of 10,000 is a simple reprint of the sixth, with the addition of Appendix B.

The Conspectus of Protestant Missions for March, 1884, which forms pages 40, 41, will be found to bring into one focus a great amount of valuable information. It shews the population of every province, the number of Protestant Missionaries in them, with the stations they occupy, and the number of workers at each station; the Societies to which the workers belong, the date of each Society's commencing work in China; and the total number of married men, single men, and single women engaged in the work. The number of British, American, and Continental Societies represented in China, and the number of Missionaries connected with each in China, as a whole, and in each station in particular, together with other useful information, may be seen at a glance. A careful study of that one table, with the aid of a map of China, will give a comprehensive view of the extent of the work of Protestant Missions in the empire. A valuable table, given as an appendix, contains the *names* of all the Protestant Missionaries, and the dates of their arrival in China, arranged under their societies and stations, and will also be found worthy of study. It also indicates by the use of various types, the proportion of Missionaries, male and female, engaged in medical work.

The statistical table given in this edition as Appendix B, reprinted from "*The Chinese Recorder*," gives a general summary of the position of Protestant Missions in China on December 31st, 1886. We trust the year 1887 will witness great additions to the number both of Missionaries and converts in connection with each branch of the work. In the CHINA INLAND MISSION we are praying for a hundred additional Missionaries during the year. By the end of February, thirty towards the hundred had been accepted by our Council. We ask prayer for special guidance in the acceptance of candidates, that only GOD-sent, fully consecrated men and women, "willing, skilful" workers, may go forth.

Many readers of this pamphlet may render invaluable service to China by diffusing the information it contains in the form of Missionary addresses. It will not be found difficult to enlarge the diagrams—on the black-board or otherwise—to illustrate such addresses, which will greatly add to their value. Above all, let us not forget that we all may serve China by prayer to GOD, without whose aid no other help would avail.

J. Hudson Taylor.

6, PYRLAND ROAD,
MILDMAY, LONDON, N.
March, 1887.

CHINA'S SPIRITUAL NEED AND CLAIMS.

"*If thou forbear to deliver them that are drawn unto death,*
"*And those that are ready to be slain;*
"*If thou sayest, Behold, we knew it not;*
"*Doth not He that pondereth the heart consider it?*
"*And He that keepeth* THY *soul, doth not He know it?*
"*And shall not He render to every man according to his works?*"
(PROV. xxiv., 11, 12.)

IT IS a solemn and most momentous truth that our every act in this present life—and our every omission too—has a direct and important bearing both on our own future welfare, and on that of others. And as believers, it behoves us to do *whatsoever* we do in the name of our LORD JESUS CHRIST. In His name, and with earnest prayer for His blessing, the following pages are written: in His name, and with earnest prayer for His blessing, let them be read. The writer feels deeply that, as a faithful steward he is bound to bring the facts contained in these pages before the hearts and consciences of the LORD'S people. He believes, too, that these facts must produce *some* fruit in the heart of each Christian reader. The legitimate fruit will undoubtedly be—not vain words of empty sympathy, but—effectual fervent prayer, and strenuous self-denying effort for the salvation of the benighted Chinese. And if in any instance they fail to produce this fruit, the writer would urge the consideration of the solemn words at the head of this page,—"If thou forbear to deliver them that are drawn unto death, and those that are ready to be slain; if thou sayest, Behold, we knew it not; doth not He that pondereth the heart consider it? and

He that keepeth *thy* soul, doth not He know it? and shall not He render to every man according to his works?"

Very early in the course of His ministry, the LORD JESUS taught His people that they were to be *the light*—not of Jerusalem, not of Judea, nor yet of the Jewish nation, but—*of the world*. And He taught them to pray—not as the heathen, who use vain and unmeaning repetitions; nor yet as the worldly-minded, who ask first and principally (if not solely) for their own private benefit and need: "For," said He, "*your* FATHER knoweth what things *ye* have need of before ye ask Him. After this manner therefore pray ye:—

"Our FATHER which art in heaven,
"Hallowed be *Thy* name;
"*Thy* kingdom come;
"*Thy* will be done; as in heaven, so in earth."

And it was only after these petitions, and quite secondary to them, that *any* personal petitions were to be offered. Even the very moderate one, "Give us *this day* our daily bread," followed them. Is not this order too often reversed in the present day? Do not Christians often really feel, and also act, as though it was incumbent upon them to *begin* with, "Give us this day our daily bread;" virtually *concluding* with, "If consistent with this, may Thy name be hallowed too?" And is not Matt. vi. 33, "Seek ye *first* the kingdom of GOD, and His righteousness; and all these things shall be *added* unto you;" practically read, even amongst the professed followers of CHRIST, Seek first all *these things* (food and clothing, health, wealth, and comfort), and *then* the kingdom of GOD and His righteousness? Instead of honouring Him with the first-fruits of our time and substance, are we not content to offer Him the fragments that remain after our own supposed need is supplied? While we thus refuse to bring the tithes into His storehouse, and to prove the LORD therewith, can we wonder that He does not open the windows of heaven, and pour us out the fulness of blessing that we desire?

We have a striking exemplification of the manner in which we should seek first the kingdom of GOD and His righteousness, in the life and in the death of our LORD JESUS CHRIST. And when risen from the dead, ere He ascended on high, He commissioned His people to make known everywhere the glad tidings of salvation—full and free—through faith in His finished work. This duty He enjoined on *us*; enjoined in the most unmistakable form, and to the most definite extent; saying, "Go YE, into ALL the world, and preach the gospel to EVERY CREATURE." Grievously has the Church failed in fulfilling this command. Sad it is to realise that so near to the close of the nineteenth century of the

Christian era, there are immense tracts of our globe either wholly destitute of, or most inadequately provided with, the means of grace and the knowledge of salvation.

Leaving other fields, however, let us concentrate our attention on the Chinese empire. Let us reflect on its great antiquity, its vast extent, its teeming population; on its spiritual destitution, and overwhelming need. Let us survey the efforts that have been put forth for its good, and contemplate the work which still remains to be done, ere the gospel is preached to "every creature" throughout this empire. And may the view we shall obtain give rise to devout gratitude to God for our own superior privileges, to humiliation before Him for our past want of earnestness in the dissemination of the truth, and to more strenuous efforts in future for China's good.

ANTIQUITY AND CIVILIZATION.

It is surely high time that this ancient and most interesting empire had the gospel fully proclaimed in its purity and soul-saving power. Long enough has it been held in the thraldom of sin and Satan. No other nation has been left for so many centuries to suffer in darkness, and to prove how utterly unable man is to raise himself without Divine revelation, and the regenerating power of the Holy Ghost. This empire, in its antiquity, stands the sole remaining relic of the hoary ages of the past, and of patriarchal times. For forty centuries it has enjoyed many of the fruits of a certain measure of civilization and of literary attainment. Our own antiquities sink into insignificance in comparison. As early as the reign of Edward the First, fire-arms were invented in China. The art of printing was discovered there in the reign of our Saxon king Athelstan. Paper was first made about A.D. 150; and gunpowder about the commencement of the Christian era. While the inhabitants of our now highly-favoured island were wandering about, painted savages, the Chinese were a settled people, living under the same form of constitutional government as they at present possess. Or to go back to times long antecedent to the history of our own country;—when Daniel foretold the rise and fall of the Persian, Grecian, and Roman empires; when at an earlier period Isaiah foretold the downfall of Babylon; or earlier still, when Jonah threatened the destruction of Nineveh—the Chinese nation was one of the greatest in the world. When Solomon reigned in Jerusalem in all his glory; when David, the sweet singer of Israel, wrote his psalms of matchless beauty; then the Chinese were enjoying many of the benefits of civilization and good government. One of their classical writings—to this day committed to memory by every advanced scholar in China—was composed by Wun-wang, an emperor who lived a century before David's reign. When Moses, learned in all the wisdom of the Egyptians, led the people of Israel from the house of bondage to the promised land, Chinese laws and literature were probably not inferior to, while their religious views were far in advance of, those of Egypt; the worship of graven images not having been introduced into China until some centuries after this period. Upwards of 200 years before the call of Abraham, certain astronomical

(Terraces for the Growth of Rice.)
CHINESE CIVILIZATION ILLUSTRATED IN AGRICULTURE.

observations were recorded by Chinese historians, which have been verified by astronomers of our own times. And the oldest record of antiquity, still possessed by the Chinese, graven on the rocks of Hung-shan some half-century antecedent to this early period, was intended to perpetuate the memory of engineering works not less remarkable for extent or difficulty than those displayed in the erection of the pyramids of Egypt. Since that time Egypt has risen to the zenith of its glory; has faded and become "the basest of the kingdoms." Since that time the once famous empires of Assyria, Babylonia, Persia, Greece, and Rome, have waxed—and waned—and passed away; but China still remains, the only monument of ages long bygone. For 4000 years this empire has been preserved by the power of God, and it shall be yet preserved until His word, delivered more than twenty-five centuries ago by the mouth of His servant Isaiah, shall be fulfilled to the last jot and tittle:—"I will make all My mountains a way, and My highways shall

WHITE MARBLE BRIDGE NEAR PEKIN.

be exalted. Behold, these shall come from far, and, lo, these from the north, and from the west, and these from the land of Sinim (China)."

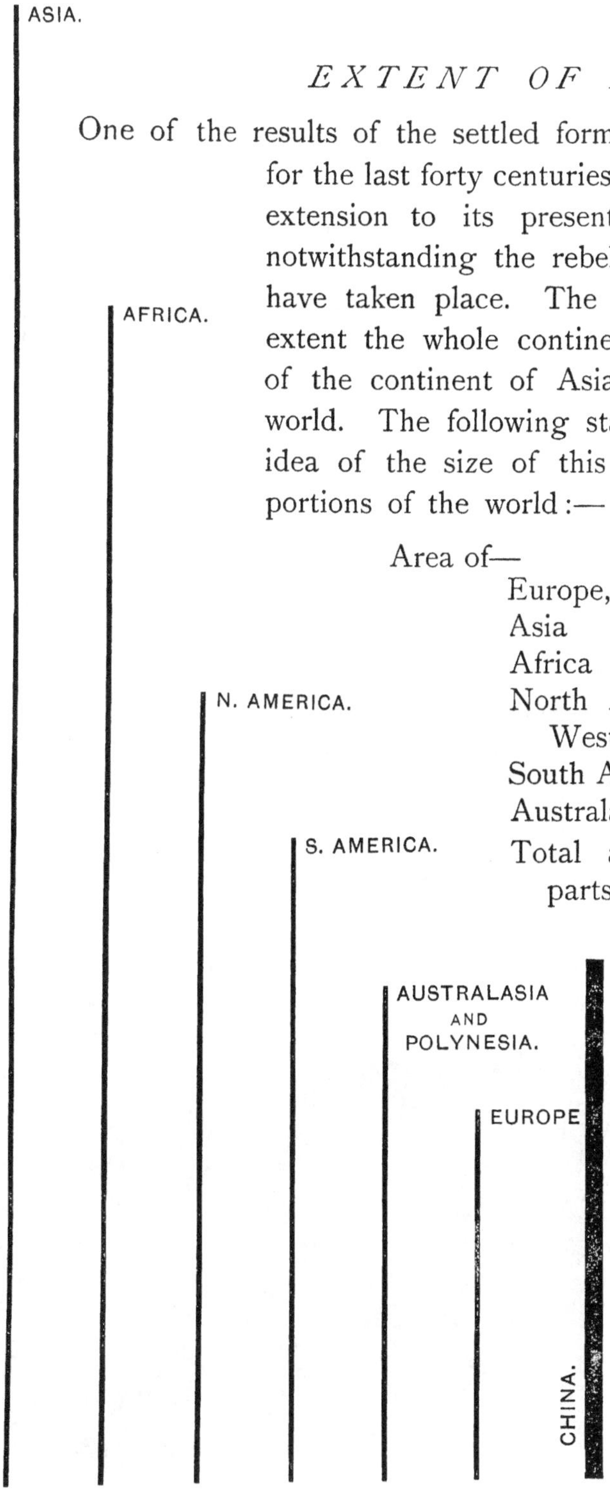

ASIA.

EXTENT OF EMPIRE.

One of the results of the settled form of government enjoyed by China for the last forty centuries, has been its gradual growth and extension to its present gigantic proportions; and this notwithstanding the rebellions and dynastic changes which have taken place. The Chinese empire, far exceeding in extent the whole continent of Europe, comprises one-third of the continent of Asia, and one-tenth of the habitable world. The following statistics will give the reader some idea of the size of this empire, as compared with other portions of the world:—

AFRICA.

Area of—	Square Miles
Europe, with its islands ...	3,797,256
Asia " ...	15,174,534
Africa " ...	11,901,274
North America, including the West Indies	7,929,231
South America, with its islands	6,410,610
Australasia and Polynesia ...	5,198,500
Total area of the habitable parts of the globe ...	50,411,405

N. AMERICA.

S. AMERICA.

CHINESE EMPIRE, 5,300,000

AUSTRALASIA AND POLYNESIA.

EUROPE

CHINA.

By way of illustrating the extent of the above continents, we give the accompanying lines, which may assist the mind to grasp their relative size. Many fail to realise how small Europe is compared with other continents; and still more are insufficiently impressed with the dimensions and importance of the Chinese empire. It will be seen from this diagram, that to benefit China means to benefit a much larger territory than Europe. Australia, vast as it is, together with Tasmania, New Zealand, and all the archipelagoes of the South Sea Islands, put together do not equal the Chinese empire in extent. Some, again, as they look at the lines representing North and South America will, perhaps, be surprised to see the extent of China in comparison. *What* must be the spiritual need and claims of a country like this?

It may further impress the mind if we take some smaller and more familiar standards of comparison: the area of the Chinese empire exceeds 44 times that of the United Kingdom of Great Britain and Ireland, 104 times that of

CHINESE EMPIRE.

Area, 5,300,000 *square miles.*

GREAT BRITAIN AND IRELAND.

Area, 120,000 *square miles.*

SCOTLAND.

Area, 30,000 *square miles.*

England alone, and 176 times that of Scotland. Could the empire of China be changed from its present form to that of a long strip of land a mile in breadth, a person walking 30 miles a day would require more than 483 years to walk from one end of it to the other. Of its area, Chinese Tartary and Thibet contain rather more than three-fifths, the remaining two-fifths being contained in China Proper.

THE GREAT WALL OF CHINA.

A STREET IN HAN-KOW.

POPULATION.

Another result of the constitutional government of China has been the steady increase and spread of its population. The Chinese have not been divided into tribes and clans, whose chief employment has been to wage war against, and to exterminate, one another. Principally occupied in the peaceful engagements of agriculture and commerce, or seeking celebrity by literary attainments, the increase of the people has had fewer checks than in most nations. As to the number of inhabitants at present contained in the whole empire, we are unable to speak with certainty. About the year 1850,

Dr. Gutzlaff stated the population of Chinese Tartary and Thibet to be as follows:—

	Estimate of 1850.		Estimate of 1884.
Manchuria	8 millions	...	8 millions
Mongolia	15 ,,	...	5 ,,
Sungaria	2 ,,	...	2 ,,
Thibet	8 ,,	...	8 ,,
Total dependencies ...	33 millions	...	23 millions

We do not know the data from which Dr. Gutzlaff derived his statistics. Since then Russia has absorbed no small part of Manchuria, but so many Chinese have emigrated into what remains, that the population may still be eight millions. The statement about the population of Mongolia was certainly too large. It is, perhaps, impossible to arrive at accuracy with regard to some of these regions, as it would be no easy matter to make a correct census of migratory Tartar hordes inhabiting the vast steppes of Central and Northern Asia. But, surely, *we* should follow them in spirit; our hearts should be moved with Christ-like compassion, when we think of them "scattered abroad as sheep having no shepherd;" and our whole souls should cry to the great Lord of the harvest to send forth labourers to seek these lost ones, that they may be saved.

As to China Proper we have fuller information. Without going over much that has been written on the subject, we may mention that in the first edition of this book we accepted the then generally assumed population of China at 400 millions. While this estimate was, perhaps, not very exessive thirty years ago, the rebellions, famines, and pestilences, which have since devastated in turn every province of the empire, have made previous estimates utterly unreliable. Moreover, the well-known effect of excessive opium-smoking (which latterly has attained to alarming proportions) on the number and vitality of the smoker's offspring, cannot be overlooked in estimating the present population of China. We do not wish to overstate the case, and to attempt to make China's need appear greater than it really is; and therefore, for our present purpose, accepting a recent, well-supported estimate of 250 millions as the basis of our calculations, assume China Proper to have 227 millions of people. If any object to this as too low, then our argument becomes all the stronger; if accepted as approximately correct, the need will still be seen to be one of overwhelming magnitude. Those specially interested in the question of the population of China, are referred for fuller information to the papers on the subject in the Appendix.

We proceed, then, on the assumption that the present population of the empire is 250 millions. How immense is this number! what mind can grasp it? We speak lightly of millions, and with very little realisation of what the vast numbers mean. If a railway train could go twelve hours without stopping to relieve the driver or to take in water, and were to travel during the twelve hours at the uniform rate of thirty miles an hour, it would make 360 miles a day. Seven years and a half of such travel, without a single day's intermission, would not accomplish *one* million miles; and had a train commenced to travel at this rate on the first day of the Christian era, and continued every day since without intermission, each day completing its quota of 360 miles, it would not yet have nearly accomplished 250 millions of miles.

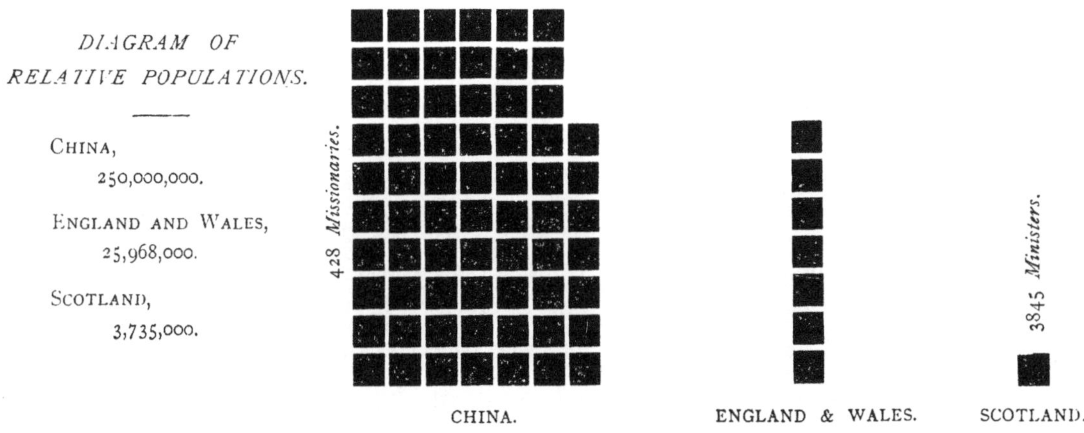

So inconceivably great a number is 250 millions, and yet this is the number of souls in China. Two hundred and fifty millions! Ten times the population of densely peopled England; or nearly sixty-seven times that of Scotland. Were the subjects of the court of Pekin marshalled in single file, allowing one yard between man and man, they would encircle the globe more than seven times at its equator. Were they to march past the spectator at the rate of thirty miles a day, they would move on and on, day after day, week after week, month after month; and over seventeen years and a quarter would elapse before the last individual passed by. Of this vast multitude, it is estimated that 22,000 are communicants in connection with Protestant missions in China. What portion of the seventeen years would it take for them to pass by? Little more than half a day would suffice! Two days and a half would permit all the attendants on Christian worship in China to pass by, while seventeen years would be required by the heathen. Mournful and impressive fact—such is the proportion of those who are journeying heavenward to those whose dark and Christless lives, if not speedily enlightened, must end in dark and Christless deaths, and—after death the judgment! Two hundred and fifty millions! an army whose numbers no finite mind can fully grasp. The number is inconceivable—the view is appalling!

Among so vast a population the number of deaths continually occurring is necessarily very great. At a very moderate computation it cannot be under 22,800 per diem, or nearly 1,000 per hour. That we may better realise what these figures represent, let us compare them with the populations of some of our well-known English towns:—

CANTERBURY has a population of	21,701
CREWE ,, ...	24,372
EASTBOURNE ,, ...	21,977
GRAVESEND ,, ...	23,375
KIDDERMINSTER ,, ...	24,270
LEAMINGTON ,, ...	22,976
LUTON ,, ...	23,959
PETERBOROUGH ,, ...	21,219
TORQUAY ,, ...	24,765
TUNBRIDGE WELLS ,, ...	24,309

None of these towns are small ones, yet the daily mortality in China would almost blot out the largest of them, and 10¼ days the whole! Think of it! Let the reader realise it if he can, for the thought is overwhelming. And can the Christians of England sit still with folded arms while these multitudes are perishing—perishing for lack of knowledge—for lack of that knowledge which England possesses so richly, which has made England what England is, and has made us what we are? What does the MASTER teach us? Is it not that if one sheep out of a hundred be lost, we are to leave the ninety and nine and seek that one? But here the proportions are almost reversed, and we stay at home with the one sheep, and take no heed to the ninety and nine perishing ones! Christian brethren, think of the imperative command of our great CAPTAIN and LEADER, "*Go*, go *ye*, into *all* the world, and preach the gospel to *every* creature;" think of the millions upon millions of poor benighted China to whom no loving follower of the self-renouncing ONE has "brought good tidings of good," or "published salvation," and weigh well the fearful words: "If *thou* forbear to deliver them that are drawn unto death, and those that are ready to be slain; if thou sayest, Behold, we knew it not; doth not He that pondereth the heart consider it? and He that keepeth *thy* soul, doth not He know it? and shall not He render to every man according to his works?"

Having thus noticed the spiritual destitution of China, let us now briefly review the efforts which have been made to introduce Christianity into this vast empire.

CHRISTIAN EFFORT.

It is exceedingly probable that even during the first century of the Christian era the gospel was preached in China. On this point we have no authentic information; but the traditions that have been handed down are probably based on facts. It is, however, well known that the Nestorians established themselves there in the 7th century, and for some time propagated their tenets under the sanction of the reigning emperors. They continued to exert some influence until the 13th or 14th century, and traces of them appear as late as the 15th century. It is probable that the form of Christianity introduced by them was from the first considerably corrupted; and as far as we can learn, the light they did possess became gradually more and more enfeebled, till there was too little life left to resist persecution or opposition from adverse rulers.

ROMISH MISSIONS

It was before the final extinction of the Nestorians that the first efforts of Rome were made in China. But little, however, was effected by its emissaries before the 16th century. During that and the following century, through the efforts of Ricci, Schaal, and their successors, the Romish missionaries made great progress. In the commencement of the 17th century, and under the enlightened emperor Kang-he, their efforts were very successful, and their influence was widely extended; but by their own dissensions, and by the assertion of the authority of the Pope, they raised the suspicions of the Chinese, and brought about their own suppression. In the persecutions subsequent to this period, many Romish missionaries laid down their lives rather than abandon their work. Within a few years, seventy French priests are said to have suffered martyrdom; while others of different nationalities, bore every conceivable torture ere death closed the scene. And never have they given up *their* hold of China. Entering by stealth, living in concealment, pursuing their labours under the greatest disadvantages, ever and anon meeting with imprisonment, sufferings, torture, and death itself, they have presented a remarkable instance of fidelity to their calling. Shall we who have the full light of the pure gospel be so much behind these men in our zeal and patience and perseverance for the spread of that gospel? Shall we prove less obedient to the command of our SUPERIOR, the LORD JESUS, and neglect *His* behest, "Go ye, into all the world, and preach the Gospel to every creature?" To our shame we must acknowledge that such has been the case hitherto. Let us confess our sin, and earnestly seek grace to wipe away the blot from the honour of our MASTER's cause.

The statistics of Romish missions in China are difficult to procure. We were able to refer in our first edition, to the fact that in 1848 they counted 34 European missionaries, 135 native priests, 14 seminaries and colleges, 326 churches and chapels, and 315,000 Chinese converts; but that since the political concessions of 1858-60, they were reported to have added to their staff about 200 European priests and sisters of charity.

In our third edition we were able to give a comparative table of Statistics of Romish and Protestant missions for 1866, which shewed the great advances they were making. They then had 33 bishops, 263 European priests, 243 native priests, 15 colleges, and 383,580 Chinese converts.

Nor have they been less active since. The Manual of the Methodist Episcopal Church of America for April, 1882, quotes from "*The Roman Catholic Register*" of Hongkong, the following statistics of Roman Catholic missions in the Chinese empire:—Bishops 41, European priests 664, native priests 559, colleges 34, convents 34, native converts 1,092,818.

PROTESTANT MISSIONS.

We are now prepared to take a survey of Protestant missions in China.

On the 7th of March, 1798, a most interesting circular, pleading for the translation and circulation of the Scriptures in the Chinese language, was sent forth, dated from 'Near Daventry, Northamptonshire,' by the Rev. William Moseley, who also issued a powerful appeal on behalf of China. There seems much reason to believe that the efforts of this earnest servant of CHRIST had a direct connection with the formation of the BRITISH AND FOREIGN BIBLE SOCIETY, and with the sending forth of Dr. Morrison to China in 1807, by the LONDON MISSIONARY SOCIETY, which had thus the honour of sending the first Protestant missionary to China. Owing to the jealousy felt by the East India Company, Dr. Morrison had to go by way of America, and arrived in Canton in 1808. In the year 1814, he published the New Testament in Chinese, about half of it being his own translation, and the remainder a revision of a manuscript found in the British Museum; and in the same year the first convert, Tsai Ako, was baptized. In 1818 the whole bible was published, the joint work of Morrison and Milne; and Dr. Marshman's version was published four years later. During the years 1817—23, Morrison's Dictionary was being compiled and carried through the press. When, in 1834, this devoted pioneer entered into his rest, the prospect of the evangelization of China was nearly as dark as when he landed twenty-seven years previously; and during that time only three additional workers had come to labour in China itself. Indeed, until the year 1842, the efforts of Protestant missionaries were for the most part of a preparatory nature. Stations had been formed in the adjacent islands, tracts and Scriptures had been translated, books had been printed and circulated, and a few converts had been made; but it was not till 1842 that China was really open to missionary effort. Canton was then worked with more efficiency, Hongkong was in our possession, and Amoy and Shanghai were opened as missionary stations. In 1844 permanent missionary work was commenced in Ningpo, and in 1846 in Foo-chow. In 1844-5-6, edicts of toleration to Christianity were issued by the Chinese emperor; and since that time the work has continued steadily, if not always rapidly, to progress.

The Church Missionary Society's first agents reached China in 1844; the two agents of the General Baptist Missionary Society arrived in 1845; the Rev. W. C. Burns, of the English Presbyterian Mission, arrived in 1848; in 1851 the Rev. George Piercy, now of the Wesleyan Missionary Society, reached China; in 1854 the writer arrived at Shanghai; and more recently, agents of other British Missionary Societies have joined in the good work. A further number of labourers has been sent forth by various American Missionary Societies, while the Continental Societies have contributed not a few earnest workers. In 1860-1, the number of Protestant missionaries in China reached 115; but in March, 1865, when the CHINA INLAND MISSION was projected, it had fallen off to about 91. Since that time many have gone out and laboured in China, and in March, 1884, there were 428 missionaries in the field, and 52 absent on furlough, giving a total of 480.

The labours of these missionaries and of their predecessors have been fruitful—more so than under the circumstances could have been expected, or even hoped for, as the following retrospect will strikingly shew. In 1833, the year before Dr. Morrison died, Dr. Wells Williams—author of the well-known treatise, "*The Middle Kingdom*"—arrived in China; and in 1834, Dr. Peter Parker arrived. Both these servants of GOD were spared to witness fifty years' progress, though not all the time in the mission field. When they arrived, Dr. Bridgman and Mr. Stevens were at Canton, where missionary operations

CANTONESE JUNKS.

could only be carried on by stealth—then the profession of CHRIST by a native was a capital crime. In the Straits of Malacca, there were six missionaries working among the Chinese, and there were *there* seven converts and one ordained native evangelist, but none were to be found in China itself. Even foreign merchants were confined to Macao, and to the factories at Canton: for exercise they could walk backwards and forwards in front of their prison-like residences, but might go no further. And no foreign *woman* was allowed to reside even there.

How great the contrast now! There are some twenty free ports open to our residence and commerce, our diplomatic representatives reside at Pekin, and men and women with proper passports may and do travel in every province of China. Protestant missions are carried on by 32 Missionary Societies (English, American, and German), and Li Hung-chang, the most influential Chinese mandarin in the empire, openly patronizes a missionary hospital, to which he is the largest contributor. There are now 1100 native helpers assisting Protestant missionaries, 22,000 communicants, and probably 100,000 Chinese, more or less fully instructed in the truth, and regularly attending Christian services. Some of the aboriginal tribes have been reached; a few of the Miao-tsï have been baptized, and the Thibetans are receiving the Scriptures in their own mother tongue. Shans and Kah-chens have been brought into the fold of the good SHEPHERD. In China 428 missionaries, connected with the 32 different societies, were at work in March, 1884. Japan is also open, and has many converts: Corea is likewise open, and has a few converts. Though these countries are not part of China, they are so closely connected with it as to merit mention here. "What hath GOD wrought!" is the grateful exclamation which a survey of the results of missionary labour calls forth.

RATE OF PROGRESS.

And not only is the progress made within the last fifty years considerable; one of the most encouraging features of the work is the steady and increasingly rapid *rate* of progress. At a Missionary Conference, held in London in March, 1884, Mr. Donald Matheson mentioned the following important facts:—

In 1853	there	were	350	native	converts	in	China
,, 1863	,,	,,	2,000	,,	,,	,,	,,
,, 1873	,,	,,	8,000	,,	,,	,,	,,
,, 1883	,,	,,	22,000	,,	,,	,,	,,

It is thus unmistakably proved that the Chinese, who so much need the gospel, are amenable to its vivifying and sanctifying influences; making the call all the more imperative to carry this blessed gospel into every corner of that vast land. Grateful we should be, grateful we are, to Almighty GOD for the triumphs of the cross already won in China; but we must not forget that the work is only begun, and very feebly begun, as yet. MUCH remains to be done before GOD's name is generally hallowed in China. MUCH, very much more must be accomplished before our SAVIOUR's command to preach the gospel to every creature is fulfilled there. If we wish to ascertain how far this command is being carried out, let us look a little more minutely at the present state and condition of this great empire; and darkness, thick darkness, will still be found to cover much of the land.

We will commence our survey with those provinces of China Proper in which missionary effort has been longest put forth. In considering the adequacy of the present staff of missionaries to the work before them, it is necessary, for argument's sake, to suppose them to occupy a definite sphere of labour. Their work is largely evangelistic, and not merely pastoral, and as many of them are assisted by a larger or smaller staff of native helpers, so their sphere may be supposed to be an extensive one. Lest we should be thought to underrate it, we will allow to each labourer 100,000 Chinese—men, women, and children—as his circle of influence; and this without considering the proportion of missionaries who, having newly arrived, have not yet acquired the language, or who from sickness, age, or infirmity, are able to accomplish less than when in their full vigour. To enable the reader to realise the number of persons we suppose each missionary to reach, the following statistics are given as a standard of comparison. On this assumption, speaking in round numbers—

BRADFORD, containing	183,032	inhabitants,	would have	2	men
BRIGHTON ,,	107,528	,,	,,	1	man
BRISTOL ,,	206,503	,,	,,	2	men
LEEDS ,,	309,126	,,	,,	3	,,
LIVERPOOL ,,	502,425	,,	,,	5	,,
MANCHESTER ,,	341,508	,,	,,	4	,,
NEWCASTLE ,,	145,225	,,	,,	2	,,
NOTTINGHAM ,,	186,656	,,	,,	2	,,
SHEFFIELD ,,	284,410	,,	,,	3	,,
EDINBURGH ,,	228,190	,,	,,	2	,,
GLASGOW ,,	511,532	,,	,,	5	,,

Such a comparison will make it sufficiently obvious that no missionary, even with the help of his native brethren, could adequately evangelize 100,000 individuals. A recent article in "*The Regions Beyond*" has so strikingly shewn the difficulty of reaching large numbers, that we quote the following paragraphs:—

"We must remember that human powers are very limited, and that the most earnest missionary can only reach a certain number with his message. No men *could* preach more frequently or to larger audiences than Messrs. Moody and Sankey, the beloved and honoured American evangelists now labouring in our great metropolis. The halls in which they preach hold about five thousand. The crowded audiences which fill them strike the mind with an overwhelming sense of the solemnity of the task of proclaiming the word of life to such a mass of human beings. Filled four times on Sunday, and nine or ten times in the week besides, sometimes with men, sometimes with women, and sometimes with mixed audiences, we may presume that in the course of each fortnight's mission to a given locality, the evangelists preach and sing the gospel to perhaps 25,000 different individuals.

"They have already completed five such missions in different parts of London, and hope to hold ten more, if the Lord permit, before they leave.

"Two halls are occupied alternately, the one being taken down and re-erected while the other is being used. No time is lost between the missions. The day after the work at Stratford ends, that at New Cross begins, and so on.

"The strain on the evangelists of thirteen such services, each lasting two hours on an average, is very great indeed. Unless they were men of iron constitution, in splendid health and spirits, they could not stand it at all; and, moreover, unless they were backed up by abundant and efficient assistance, even their tremendous energies could not accomplish a tithe of what they do accomplish. The movement happily *is* thus backed up. Active and competent helpers of one sort or other may be reckoned by the hundred. Committee-men and secretaries; choir leaders and choirs; assistant preachers and Christian workers; ladies and gentlemen; ministers and young converts; all help to water the word and bring in the sheaves, whilst money almost *ad libitum* is freely forthcoming that the people may hear the gospel. Architects, contractors, writers, advertisers, bill distributors, &c., &c., also lend their help, while thousands the world over are praying for a blessing.

"Yet with all this stupendous amount of *united* effort, and all this freely consecrated wealth, with the unique and remarkable gifts of the evangelists themselves, and the rich blessing of God poured upon their labours, what is the utmost the movement can accomplish in the way of reaching the population of the metropolis?

"Fifteen separate missions, in widely different parts of London, will *each* affect say 25,000, and the whole campaign consequently 375,000. If it extend to *sixteen* separate missions, then 400,000 persons may hear the message of salvation from these evangelists. This is the utmost that can be hoped for as regards numbers, and may justly be considered a glorious result of the work of *one year*, the rest of which must needs be more or less devoted to rest.

"But 400,000 is not one-tenth part of the population of London and its suburbs, which is reckoned now at about *five millions*.

"It would, therefore, take Messrs. Moody and Sankey, and their fellow-workers of every description, *twelve years* of such intense, arduous, unremitting, and united labour, to carry the gospel to *all* the people living in London and its suburbs, and it would cost moreover a fabulous sum of money!

"Nor is that all! The inhabitants of London are all nominal Christians to begin with; they can all read; they all have the Bible, they all have some knowledge, however defective, of its contents. Mr. Moody can freely speak to them of the love of God without stopping to explain what love is, or that God is not a bit of painted and gilded wood. He can allude to the good Samaritan or the prodigal son without pausing to tell the stories. He has only to put a finishing touch as it were to a work already more than half done. Other men laboured, and he enters into their labours. Christian mothers, Christian teachers, Christian friends, Christian books and papers, Christian laws and customs, Christian preachers and teachers, have already enlightened the mind and awakened the conscience, and prepared the way of the Lord in the souls to which Mr. Moody preaches and Mr. Sankey sings; and they will continue to water the word when the evangelists are gone. Give them, on the contrary, an audience as unprepared as the crowd that gathers in the street of a Chinese town or an African market-place, and what would they accomplish by a fortnight's meetings?

"Nor is that all! Moody speaks and Sankey sings to men and women in their own tongue wherein they were born. What if they had first to acquire, and then, with difficulty and many a blunder, to use a foreign idiom? and what, if that idiom, even when fully acquired, contained no words expressive of such ideas as goodness, holiness, love, peace, purity, heaven, or even of His character, according to our conception of the Divine being?

"If it would take the evangelists and all their friends twelve years to evangelize London—and that giving only a fortnight's meetings to each section—how long would it take them effectually to evangelize a similar population of heathen Chinese or Africans?

"They could not do it effectually in the term of their natural lives! And what if one or two men had to attempt it without friend or helper of any kind, and in spite of adverse climate and bad health, and poverty and loneliness, and every conceivable discouragement?"

We will now resume our argument. There are, as is well known, eighteen provinces in China Proper. As we cannot expect all our readers to be familiar with their extent and position, we would venture to suggest their reference to the map of China, as they follow our remarks. It will be seen that six of the provinces are on the sea-border; and that of the remaining twelve, HU-PEH is the most central. In these seven provinces, as we have mentioned, 91 Protestant missionaries were to be found from England, America, and Germany in 1865, when the China Inland Mission was formed. That number gave an average of 13 labourers to each of the seven provinces. In March, 1884, however, the number was 355* (272 men and 83 women), nearly 51 missionaries to each province. This may seem at first sight a good and fairly adequate supply; but let us now look at them more particularly.

THE SEVEN PROVINCES.

KWANG-TUNG; area 90,230 *square miles, population* 17½ *millions.*

We will commence our review with KWANG-TUNG, of which Canton is the capital. Protestant missions commenced here as we have seen in 1808; and were prosecuted more vigorously after China was opened by treaty in 1842. It has now eleven mission stations, including Canton, the British colony of Hong-kong, and Swatow. In these stations there were 55 missionaries labouring in 1884, together with 18 single ladies, making a total of 73: out of the 73 there are 57 residing in the three cities above named. The city of Canton, in which 25 of them reside, is very large, being equal in population to Liverpool, Manchester, and Brighton together; and we need scarcely say their number is all too small to work it efficiently. But if Canton is not too well supplied, what then of the other 16½ millions scattered over the province? Its extent

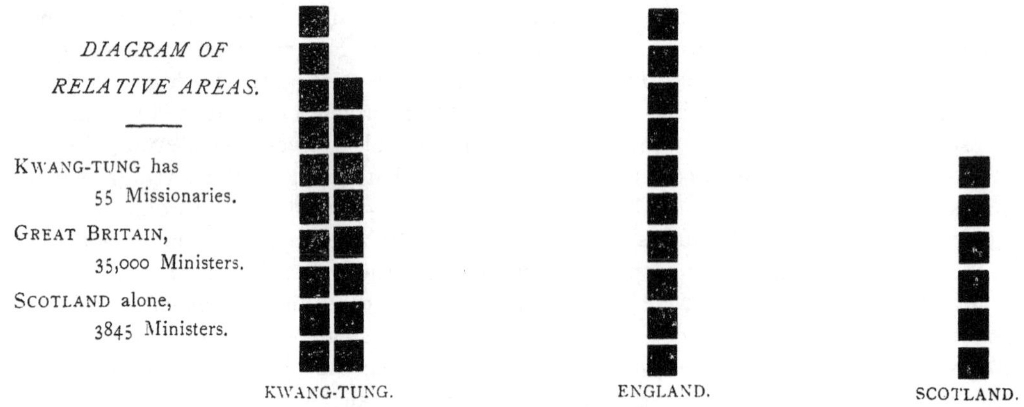

will be all the better realised by the aid of the above diagrams, which shew the relative areas of Kwang-tung, England, and Scotland. And for comparison we give at the side the numbers of male missionaries in Kwang-tung, and the number of ordained ministers in Great Britain, and in Scotland alone. Suppose all the 55 male missionaries to be distributed so as each to be the centre of influence to 100,000 Chinese, they would only suffice to proclaim CHRIST over one-third of the length and breadth of this one province of 17½ millions;

* This number excludes two, whose head-quarters are in HU-PEH, but who work in HO-NAN and HU-NAN respectively.

STREET IN CANTON.

twelve millions would never hear the glad tidings of great joy. And yet KWANG-TUNG has more missionaries in it than any other province.

FUH-KIEN; area 45,753 *square miles, population* 10 *millions.*

Proceeding up the China Sea, we next come to the province of FUH-KIEN. This province is larger than Denmark with Iceland; and is about half the size of the preceding one. It contains about 10 millions of precious souls. Foo-chow, Shao-wu and Amoy are its mission stations, with two others on the Island of Formosa. There were in March, 1884, 37 missionaries labouring in these stations, besides nine single ladies. Though better supplied with missionaries than any other province in China in proportion to its population, even here the ratio is less than that of one male missionary to a quarter of a million; or 15 labourers to a population equalling that of Scotland. And it is not too much to say that very many of the people are still utterly destitute of the gospel; and must die unreached unless more missionary effort is put forth.

TEMPLE IN RIVER MIN, NEAR FOO-CHOW.

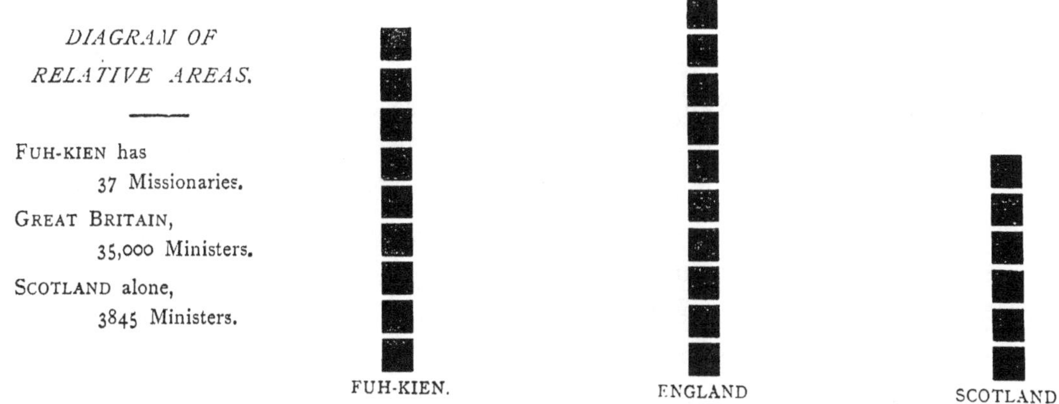

The above diagram shews FUH-KIEN to be little less than England in area, and much larger than Scotland. When the ministerial supply is compared, the contrast is seen to be painfully striking.

CHEH-KIANG; area 35,654 *square miles, population* 12 *millions.*

To the north of FUH-KIEN lies the province of CHEH-KIANG; in area the smallest in China. It is about twice the size of Greece, and contains say 12 millions of inhabitants. It has eight mission stations, in four of which the missionaries of the C.I.M. only reside. The number of missionaries labouring in the province in March, 1884, was 31, exclusive of 13 unmarried ladies, or 44 in all; of whom 34 live in three cities; and while they work around them, and sometimes take long missionary journeys, there are scores of cities and large towns without the gospel.

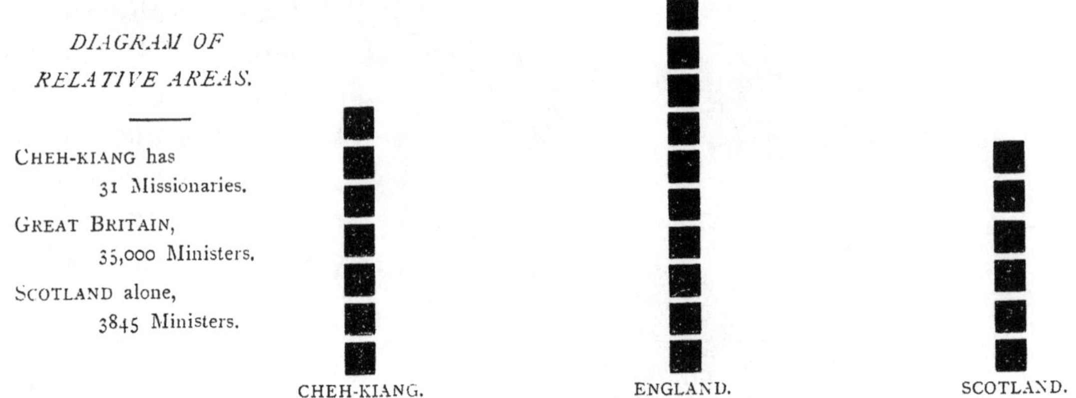

Here again, as will be seen from the above diagram, a considerable number *may* hear it if they will; but the mass still remain unsought, untaught, unsaved,—without the truth, without CHRIST, without hope, without heaven.

KIANG-SU; area 40,140 *square miles, population* 20 *millions.*

Still proceeding up the China Sea, the next province northward is KIANG-SU. Larger than the preceding province, it is three times the area of Switzerland. It is of amazing fertility, and carries on an extensive commerce. That magnificent river the Yang-tse-kiang (the great artery of the empire), and the Grand Canal, run through its midst. It is, therefore, well able to sustain its vast population of 20 millions; more than double the population of Scotland and Ireland together. Shanghai and five other stations had in 1884, besides 15 single ladies, 53 labourers for CHRIST, making a total of 68; and they are publishing to some extent the glad tidings of peace in the cities and towns around them, as well as in their own stations. But 40 of the 68 are located in Shanghai; some of whom are printers, some wholly occupied with English work; and many are almost wholly engaged in teaching schools. Of the remaining 28 missionaries, 14 are located in two cities, of the estimated population of 500,000 inhabitants each. Can these 14 workers—one of them a lady—have much spare time for work beyond their own cities and suburbs? Excluding them, and residing in three different stations, we have only 14 workers left for the remainder of a province three times as large as Switzerland. They have two large and populous cities, and one large town, in which they are stationed, to work before they think of the 18 millions scattered over the face of the province.

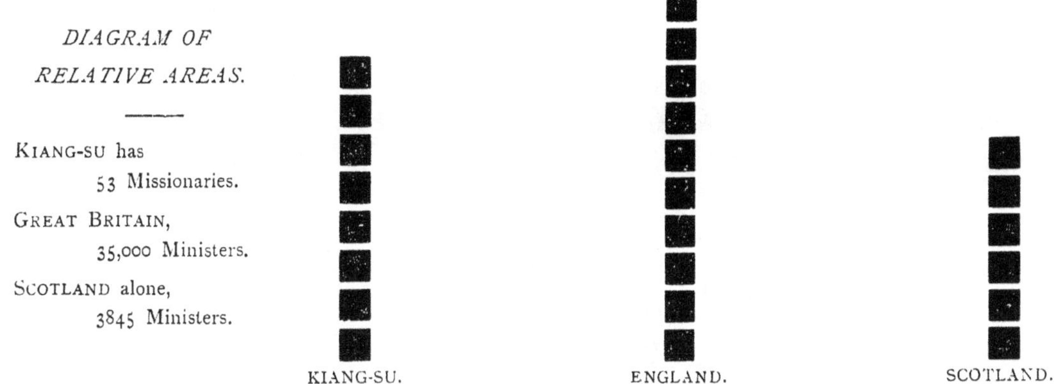

This province it will be seen is intermediate in area between Scotland and England, but has only 53 male missionaries to compare with the tens of thousands of ministers in Great Britain.

SHAN-TUNG; area 53,768 *square miles, population* 19 *millions.*

Immediately to the north of KIANG-SU lies the province of SHAN-TUNG, which is as large as Scotland, Ireland, and half of Wales. Its population may be 19 millions, and the present number of labourers is 46 all told. Ten of these workers are ladies, and another is only working among the English-speaking residents in the province; while of the remaining 35, seven are medical missionaries, and some are largely occupied with educational work.

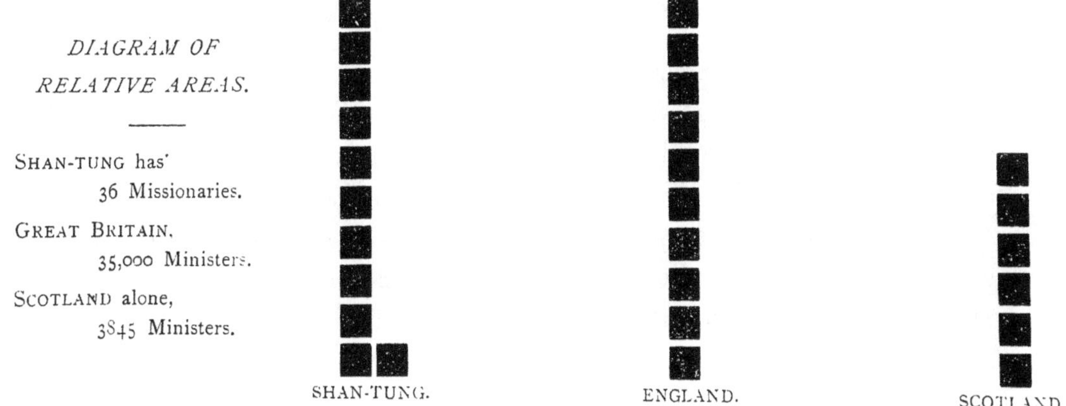

Valuable as this is, it precludes those engaged in it from any widespread evangelistic efforts. Thus we find not more than one missionary free for purely evangelistic work to each million of the people spread through the province. Might not the mass of this open, easily accessible, and healthy province truthfully exclaim, "No man careth for our souls!" The gospel has not yet been preached to "every creature" here.

CONFUCIAN TEMPLE, PEKIN.

CHIH-LI; area 67,276 *square miles, population* 20 *millions.*

Still going north we come to the province of CHIH-LI. This province is larger than England and Wales, and is now estimated to contain 20 millions of souls. Pekin, the capital of the empire; Pao-ting Fu, the capital of the province; and Tien-tsin, its principal seaport; with T'ung-chau, and Kalgan (a trading city on the Mongolian border), are its five mission stations. There were 55 missionaries in these stations in March, 1884; but what are they among so many? Imagine England with only 55 ministers of CHRIST, and that number living in five only of our cities, while all the rest were left destitute! But of these 55 missionaries four are medical men; one superintends the mission press and the secular affairs of his mission; one is a colporteur of the National Bible Society of Scotland; and 17 are single ladies, of whom four are qualified medical practitioners. Thus there are only 32 ministers of CHRIST free to give themselves exclusively to evangelistic labour in a province containing 20 millions of souls. It is easy to talk of 20 millions; but who can realise what that vast number implies? One million is a large number! "If you had a million shillings to count one by one, and did it as fast as you could for ten hours a day, it would take a fortnight; and the million shillings would weigh nearly five tons, or be a heavy load for a railway truck." But here we have not shillings but precious souls; and not one million but twenty millions of souls, who *must live for ever*, either in happiness or woe—and who can estimate the value of one soul? So priceless is the treasure that heaven and earth in all their material splendour are not to be compared to it. What then is the value of a thousand souls?—of a thousand thousand? —nay of twenty times a thousand thousand? Such is the population of this single province—six times that of Scotland; and the great mass of them are still "without hope, without GOD, and in the world."

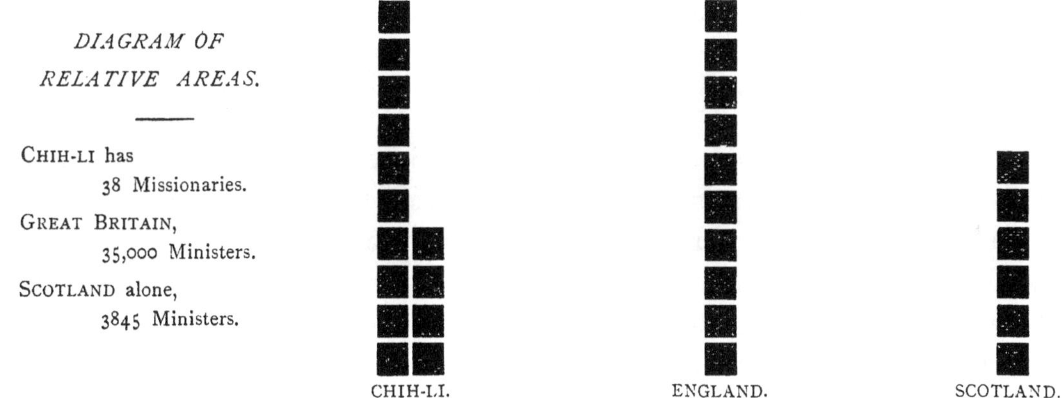

Scotland has its bibles, its psalm books, and its catechisms; its Sunday school teachers, its elders, its tract distributors; its city missionaries, and its bible-women; and besides these there are *some thousands* of Christian ministers, and yet there is not one labourer too many. CHIH-LI, with six times Scotland's population, has 32 ministers and 23 other workers!

HU-PEH; area 69,479 *square miles, population* 20½ *millions.*

The last of the seven provinces to which we have alluded is HU-PEH, which exceeds in extent one-third of France, while its population may be 20½ millions. Twenty-three* missionaries, residing in five stations (including two medical missionaries, one colporteur, and one single lady) are trying to dissipate

* Excluding two, in Fan-ch'eng and Sha-shï, who work in HO-NAN and HU-NAN.

the darkness around them. At the ratio of one man to a hundred thousand Chinese, 200 would be needed for this province alone! Who shall tell the mass of this people of a SAVIOUR's love? Who shall minister to their souls' need?

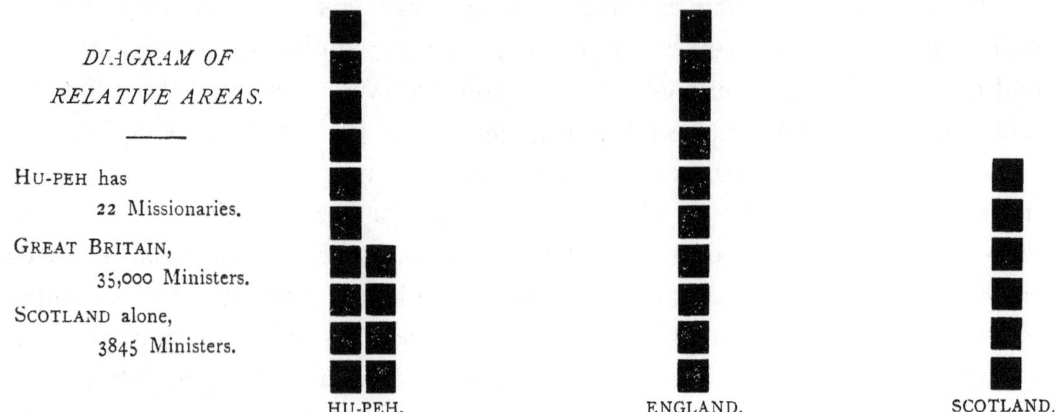

The LORD said, "Go *ye*." The Word still says, "Go *ye*." Christian brothers, Christian sisters, does not that "*ye*" mean *you?*—you who are created in CHRIST JESUS *unto good works*—a peculiar people *zealous* of good works?

SUMMARY OF THE SEVEN PROVINCES.

Looking on the state of the seven provinces now enumerated, the only provinces in which Protestant missionaries were labouring before 1865, there is an aggregate of perhaps 119 millions, of whom, allowing a hundred thousand souls to every missionary, there still remain over 80 millions, for whose direct benefit nothing is being attempted, to whom no herald of mercy is designated, and by whom the glad tidings of great joy have never been heard. Over eighty millions famishing for want of that food which GOD has so liberally provided; perishing for lack of that knowledge which it is the Church's duty to diffuse. Perishing, we say,

> While we whose souls are lighted
> With wisdom from on high,
> To CHINA's sons benighted,
> The lamp of life deny!

In 1857, the writer had on one occasion been preaching in Ningpo the glad tidings of salvation through the finished work of CHRIST, when a middle-aged man stood up, and before his assembled countrymen gave the following testimony to the power of the gospel:—"I have long sought for the truth—as did my father before me—but I have not found it. I have travelled far, but I have not found it. I have found no rest in Confucianism, Buddhism, Taoism; but I do find rest in what I have heard to-night. Henceforth

FAN-CH'ENG AND SIANG-YANG FU IN HU-PEH.

I believe in JESUS." This man was one of the leading officers of a sect of reformed Buddhists in Ningpo. A short time after this profession of faith in the SAVIOUR, there was a meeting of the sect over which he had formerly presided. The writer accompanied him to that meeting, and there, to his former co-religionists, he testified of the peace which he had obtained in believing. Soon after, one of his former companions was converted and baptized. Both now sleep in JESUS. The first of these two, long continued to preach to his countrymen the glad tidings of great joy. A few nights after his conversion, he asked the writer how long these glad tidings had been known in England. He was told that we had had the gospel for some hundreds of years. The man looked amazed. "What!" said he, "is it possible that for hundreds of years you have had the knowledge of these glad tidings in your possession, and yet have only now come to preach them to us? My father sought after the truth for more than twenty years, and died without finding it. Why did you not come sooner?" Ah! why, indeed, did we not go sooner? Why? Shall we say the way was not open? For fifty years it has been more open than we have been ready to occupy. And now that it is so much more open than ever before, why are we still so slow to enter in? Since the treaty of Tien-tsin, more *new* Romish missionaries and sisters of charity have been poured into China than the whole staff of Protestant missionaries. Why are we doing so little? While we hang back the multitudes perish.

Briefly to recapitulate our survey of the seven provinces, we find:—

PROVINCE.	AREA.	POPULATION.	MISSIONARIES.
1. KWANG-TUNG ...	90,230 square miles ...	17½ millions ...	55 men 18 women
2. FUH-KIEN ...	45,753 " " ...	10 " ...	37 " 9 "
3. CHEH-KIANG ...	35,654 " " ...	12 " ...	31 " 13 "
4. KIANG-SU ...	40,140 " " ...	20 " ...	53 " 15 "
5. SHAN-TUNG ...	53,768 " " ...	19 " ...	36 " 10 "
6. CHIH-LI ...	67,276 " " ...	20 " ...	38 " 17 "
7. HU-PEH ...	69,479 " " ...	20½ " ...	22 " 1 "
TOTALS	402,300 " " ...	119 " ...	272 men 83 women

The average population of these provinces is 17 millions, and the average number of missionaries is 51. And after allowing a far larger sphere to each missionary than he can possibly fill, and allowing a similar sphere of 100,000 souls to each single lady missionary, there still remain more than 83 millions of that interesting but benighted people in these provinces alone, utterly and hopelessly beyond the reach of the existing agencies in China for the spread of the gospel.

But deplorable as is the view thus presented by the seven provinces where missionaries have longest laboured, the prospect furnished by the rest of the empire is still more distressing, as a very brief survey will shew.

THE LAST ELEVEN PROVINCES.

Kiang-si and Gan-hwuy.

Commencing with KIANG-SI, which was first occupied by the American Methodist Episcopal Mission, and in which the C.I.M. has worked since 1869, there is a province twice the size of Portugal, and containing 15 millions of souls. It has two mission stations and five missionaries. Adjoining it, is the province of GAN-HWUY, rather smaller than England, and containing now some nine millions of people, and eight missionaries—four of whom are ladies. The C.I.M. worked there alone fifteen years; but at last one American missionary has come, and we hope that others will soon follow. Considering the work of the ladies as local, we find only nine men to evangelize these two large provinces, through which the Yang-tse passes, and steamers up and down daily convey their passengers. When will the 24 millions of these provinces *hear* the gospel of the grace of GOD?

Ho-nan and Shan-si.

In the north-west of GAN-HWUY lies the province of HO-NAN, as large as England and Wales, and containing 15 millions of inhabitants. Through GOD's blessing on the itinerant work of the C.I.M., several persons have been converted and baptized. A station, with one married missionary, resident at Ju-ning Fu, had to be given up for a time, through a local rebellion, and itineration resumed. Now there is a native helper there, and the prospect of re-opening the station. North of HO-NAN is the province of SHAN-SI, nearly as large as England and Wales. It was fearfully devastated by the famine, but still probably contains nine millions. It has now two stations and 18 missionaries (including four single ladies, and three young men who are acquiring the language). Ten of them belong to the CHINA INLAND MISSION, and one lady, unconnected, works with them. About 300 converts have been gathered by them at their stations and out-stations. The two Baptist missionaries have also some converts at T'ai-yüen Fu. The American Board Mission have five missionaries, who will probably open some new stations when they are able. In these two large provinces, therefore, there are 24 millions of souls, and only fifteen men living and working among them. Comment is needless!

Shen-si and Kan-suh.

West of SHAN-SI, and separated from it by the Yellow River, is the province of SHEN-SI, equal in extent to Holland, Saxony, Bavaria, and

Wurtemberg together. Desolated by the Mohammedan rebellion, and having suffered fearfully from the famine, it has yet probably seven millions of souls. The CHINA INLAND MISSION has 4 brethren and 6 sisters in 2 stations, occasionally itinerating in the province, and some 90 converts have been baptized, of whom (excluding cases of removal and discipline) 50 are in communion in the province. Still further west lies the vast province of KAN-SUH. The modern province is very large; far more extensive than the ancient one, which is still delineated on most English maps. It will be remembered that France is nearly four times the size of England; and that Spain is not much less than France. But KAN-SUH is larger than both France and Spain put together, and contains perhaps three millions of precious souls—a small number compared with its former population, but still far more than the whole island of Madagascar. The C.I.M. has two married missionaries, and one single sister, working there, in the only mission station in this extensive region. No Protestant missionary of any other Society has ever been stationed either in this province or in SHEN-SI. A few Christians have been gathered in KAN-SUH also. In KAN-SUH and SHEN-SI there are two immense regions, containing probably 10 millions of souls—Chinese, Thibetans, Mongols, &c., &c., and six men, four missionaries' wives, and a few single sisters alone are resident and itinerant among them to witness for the LORD JESUS! In the face of facts like these, can we consistently profess ourselves to be *believers* in the Bible, and *servants* of the Crucified ONE, whose parting word of command was—Preach "in all the world"—"to every creature?"

AGRICULTURAL LABOURERS IN SÏ-CH'ÜEN.

Sï-ch'üen and Yün-nan.

South of KAN-SUH lies SÏ-CH'ÜEN, almost bordering on Assam, and nearly as large as Sweden. The population is probably 20 millions. The C.I.M. has worked in Chung-k'ing, the commercial capital of this province, since 1877; and has gathered a small church there; and the colporteurs of the British and Foreign Bible Society, and of the National Bible Society of Scotland have made its mission premises their head-quarters when in Sï-CH'ÜEN. In January, 1882, the C.I.M. commenced work in Chen-tu, the political capital, and here also it has had the joy of baptizing a few converts. In the autumn of 1882, the American Methodist Episcopal Mission began work in Chung-k'ing, and now has four missionaries there. The C.I.M. has now eight missionaries in the two stations; and the National Bible Society of Scotland also has one European colporteur in the province. Of the total of 13 missionaries in this vast province, five are single ladies. If the eight men do their duty to the two cities in which they reside, the populations of which are not far from those of Manchester and Liverpool respectively, how much time or strength will remain for the rest of the province, which includes in its domain the large districts of Eastern Thibet? South of Sï-CH'ÜEN, lies the province of YÜN-NAN (bordering on Burmah and near to Assam), a province as large as England and Wales. It has five millions of people probably, and in Yün-nan Fu, the capital, in Ta-li Fu, the old Mohammedan capital, and in Bhamô, on the Irrawaddy in Upper Burmah, the C.I.M. has six missionaries working. We cannot say how many different tribes, speaking distinct languages—as the Thibetans, Lo-los, Shans, Kah-chens, Ming-kia, Miao-tsï among others—are to be found, not to speak of the Chinese; and there are six brethren among them all, including Mr. Henry Soltau in Bhamô. In these two provinces, therefore, covering together an area of 307,513 square miles, and containing 25 millions of precious souls, there are only 19 Protestant missionaries, fourteen of them men! one man, if you will, to 21,965 square miles of hill and dale, of mountain and valley—a district over two-thirds the size of Scotland. When could he traverse such a district, and reach the countless inhabitants it contains, even if the work of the city, in which he resides, were not in itself far more than he could possibly accomplish? Yet all these people

MR. G. W. CLARKE'S MISSION HOUSEHOLD AT TA-LI FU.

must die; daily many of them *are dying*, and dying in sin, with no knowledge of the *only* SAVIOUR; and after death the judgment! If we do not care to think of *their* judgment, is it not well that we should think of *our own?* "Am I my brother's keeper?"

MOHAMMEDAN CEMETERY NEAR TA-LI FU.

Kwei-chau, Kwang-si and Hu-nan.

There still remain three provinces, which may be taken together. In KWEI-CHAU, east of YÜN-NAN, larger than Belgium, Saxony, Hanover and Bavaria—population, four millions—the C.I.M. has one station and three missionaries—two of them still learning the language. KWANG-SI, also east of YÜN-NAN, and bordering on Tong-king, nearly equals England and Scotland in extent, and has five millions of people, but NO MISSIONARY! (One designated by the C.I.M. is gaining experience to commence work in this difficult province). HU-NAN, nearly one-third the size of Austria, has 16 millions of souls, and the C.I.M. only has one missionary itinerating among them! (Another is learning the language to assist him). The area of these three provinces together is 227,828 square miles, over seven times that of Scotland; the aggregate population is 25 millions, nearly seven times that of Scotland; and there are only the four C.I.M. missionaries among them, and two others designated. Some of these workers are often cast down and discouraged, for want of companionship and help—living alone in these vast regions and among these 25 millions! Is it not time we cried mightily to the great LORD of the harvest, to succour the lonely ones, and to send forth more labourers into HIS great harvest field? Help us, Christian friends, by your prayers!

SUMMARY OF THE ELEVEN PROVINCES.

In these eleven provinces, each averaging nearly 10 millions of population, we see a total of 108 millions of our fellow-creatures, for whose good only 29 married and 19 single men, and 20 lady missionaries are labouring. In one, KWANG-SI, no one is unfurling the standard of the cross! No one is pointing them to the great SIN-BEARER! If we aggregate all the workers in these 11 provinces, and allow to each 100,000 people as his or her sphere of labour, there will remain over 100 millions without missionary supply. Add to them the 83 millions beyond the reach of the gospel in the seven provinces first mentioned, and we have an aggregate exceeding 183 millions absolutely without those tidings which the SAVIOUR so long ago commanded to be carried to EVERY CREATURE. My Christian reader, are you quite sure that it is not *your* duty to carry the gospel to these perishing ones?

To tabulate these parts then, we find in March, 1884, there were:—

PROVINCE.	AREA.	POPULATION.	MISSIONARIES.
1. KIANG-SI ...	61,580 square miles ...	15 millions ...	Only 5 men and 0 women
2. GAN-HWUY ...	54,002 " " ...	9 " ...	" 4 " " 4 "
3. HO-NAN ...	66,928 " " ...	15 " ...	" 1* " " 0 "
4. SHAN-SI ...	65,950 " " ...	9 " ...	" 14 " " 4 "
5. SHEN-SI ...	81,215 " " ...	7 " ...	" 4 " " 6 "
6. KAN-SUH ...	166,000 " " ...	3 " ...	" 2 " " 1 "
7. SÏ-C'HÜEN ...	185,052 " " ...	20 " ...	" 8 " " 5 "
8. YÜN-NAN (including Bhamô) ...	122,461 " " ...	5 " ...	" 6 " " 0 "
9. KWEI-CHAU ...	66,758 " " ...	4 " ...	" 3 " " 0 "
10. KWANG-SI ...	77,856 " " ...	5 " ...	NONE " 0 "
11. HU-NAN ...	83,214 " " ...	16 " ...	" 1* " " 0 "
TOTALS	1,031,016 " "	108 "	Only 48 men and 20 women

RESCUE THE PERISHING.

Many years ago the following incident occurred as the writer of these pages was journeying to Sung-kiang Fu, a large city in the province of KIANG-SU, and is quoted from a journal written about the time.

"In the afternoon of the second day its walls loomed in sight, and I spoke of going ashore to preach the gospel. In the same boat was a Chinaman as passenger, who had been in England; and who, when there, went by the name of Peter. He had heard the gospel, but had not experienced its saving power. I had been speaking to him on the preceding evening about his soul's salvation, and he had been moved to

* In the Conspectus, page 41, these two workers are classed under their head-quarters, Fan-ch'eng and Sha-shï, in HU-PEH.

tears. I was pleased, therefore, when he asked to be allowed to accompany me, and to hear me preach. Our boat drew nearer the walls of the city, and I went into the cabin to prepare for going ashore, expecting in a few minutes to enter Sung-kiang Fu with my Chinese friend.

"I was suddenly startled by a splash and a cry. I sprang out of the cabin, and looked around—every one was at his post but poor Peter. The tide was rapidly running out, but a strong wind was carrying us over it. The low, shrubless shore afforded no landmark that we could notice to indicate the exact spot where he fell into the water. I instantly let down the sail and leapt overboard, trying to find him. Unsuccessful, I looked around in agonizing suspense, and saw close to me a fishing-boat with a peculiar drag-net furnished with hooks, which I knew would bring him up.

"'Come!' I cried, as hope sprang up in my heart, 'Come, and drag over this spot directly, for a man is drowning here.'

"'Veh bin'—it's not convenient—was the cold and unfeeling reply.

"'Don't talk of convenience,' I cried in an agony, 'a man is drowning!'

"'We are busy fishing and cannot come,' was the reply.

"'Never mind your fishing,' I cried, 'I will give you more money than many a day's fishing will bring you, if you will come at once.'

"'How much money will you give us?'

"'Don't stand talking now; do come, or you will be too late. I'll give you five dollars (then worth £1 13s. 4d.)'

"'We won't come for that; we'll drag for twenty dollars.'

"'I have not got so much; do come quickly, and I'll give you all the money I have.'

"'How much is that?'

"'I don't know exactly; about fourteen dollars.'

"At last they came, and in less than one minute brought up the body of poor Peter. They were most indignant and clamorous because the payment of their exorbitant demand was delayed while attempts were being made at resuscitation. But all was in vain—life was extinct."

My reader, would you not say that these men were verily guilty of this poor Chinaman's death, in that they had the means of saving him at hand, but would not use them? Surely they were! And yet, pause ere you give your judgment against them, lest a greater than Nathan say, "Thou art the man." Is it so hard-hearted, so wicked a thing to neglect to save the body? of how much sorer punishment is he worthy who leaves the soul to perish, and Cain-like says, "Am I my brother's keeper?" The Lord Jesus commands, commands *you*, my brother, and *you*, my sister. "Go," says He, "Go into *all* the world, and preach the gospel to *every* creature." Will you say to *Him*, "No, it is not convenient?" will you tell *Him* that you are busy fishing and cannot go? that you have bought a piece of ground and cannot go? that you have purchased five yoke of oxen, or have married a wife, or are engaged in other and more interesting pursuits, and cannot go? Ere long "we must all appear before the judgment seat of Christ, that every one may receive the things done in the body." Remember, oh! remember, pray for, labour for, the unevangelized Chinese; *or you will sin against your own soul.* Consider Who it is that has said, "If thou forbear to deliver them that are drawn unto death, and those that are ready to be slain; if thou sayest, Behold, we knew it not; doth not He that pondereth the heart consider it? and He that keepeth *thy* soul, doth not He know it? and shall not He render to every man according to his works?"

THE DEPENDENCIES OF CHINA.

Having completed our survey of China Proper, we must now cross the border, and cast a passing glance at the extensive, though thinly-populated regions of Chinese Tartary and Thibet. We fear lest our readers should weary of these details; but though they may seem uninteresting, they are really important and solemn realities. Whether interesting to us or not, every individual of the millions of China, every inhabitant of these vast regions, must either live for ever or die for ever. They are in a fallen state, are unclean, unthankful, unholy. Every day tens of thousands, every three months 2,000,000 subjects of the Chinese Emperor pass into eternity, very few of them ever having heard the gospel. Do we realise what this number means? A million days are 2730 years; a little more than two million days ago Adam was walking alone in the garden of Eden, and Eve was not yet formed. So large a number is two million days. But as many souls die without the gospel every three months. Should we say, "Behold, we knew it not," God will not justify our leaving them to perish on the ground of that excuse. Very uninteresting to the priest descending from Jerusalem to Jericho was the state of the poor Jew, whom the robbers had left naked, wounded, and half dead. Not so, however, to the good Samaritan; he felt the greatest interest in the case, and he shewed it too. Oh! let us shew our interest in these sin-sick, perishing souls, by making strenuous efforts to bring them to the Great Physician.

In order to enable our readers to realise the vast extent of the outlying districts of the Chinese empire, we would suggest a comparison of them with those countries which are nearer home. We have already referred to France as being nearly four times as large as England; Spain and Portugal together are considerably larger than France. But for the purpose of comparison, Great Britain and Ireland, France, Spain, and Portugal taken together do not suffice. The peninsula of Norway and Sweden is about six times as large as England; and Denmark, Iceland, and Holland exceed in extent Scotland and Ireland. Add these to the preceding, however, and the whole is still too small. Belgium, Switzerland, and Italy, may be added; Germany and Austria, and Turkey and Greece may also be added; and the sum total of all these countries does not half equal the extent of the outlying regions of the Chinese empire with which we are comparing them. Russia in Europe is about ten times as large as Spain and Portugal, and exceeds in extent the sum of all the other countries in Europe. Add this immense country to all the others we have enumerated, and we gain a more adequate standard of comparison. The whole continent of Europe has an area of 3,797,256 square miles; Manchuria, Mongolia, the North-Western Dependencies, and Thibet, together have an area of 3,951,130 square miles. These extensive regions contain many millions of our fellow creatures, but except the four missionaries in New-chwang, they have NO MISSIONARY. They are perishing, and they are left to perish. Among them NO MISSIONARY resides to make known that wisdom, the merchandise of which "is better than the merchandise of silver, and the gain thereof than fine gold." Throughout this immense territory, larger than the whole continent of Europe, with the exception noted above, there is not a single ambassador for CHRIST from all the Protestant churches in Europe and America to carry the word of reconciliation, and to pray men in CHRIST'S stead, "Be ye reconciled to GOD." How long shall this state of things be allowed to continue?

My reader, think of the over 80 millions beyond the reach of the gospel in the seven provinces where missionaries have longest laboured; think of the over 100 millions in the other eleven provinces of China Proper, beyond the reach of the few missionaries labouring there; think of the over 20 millions who inhabit the vast regions of Manchuria, Mongolia, Thibet, and the North-Western Dependencies, which exceed in extent the whole of Europe—an aggregate of over 200 millions beyond the reach of all existing agencies—and say, how shall

GOD'S name be hallowed by them,
HIS kingdom come among them, and
HIS will be done by them?

His name, His attributes, they have never heard. His kingdom is not proclaimed among them. His will is not made known to them. Do you *believe* that each unit of these millions has a precious soul? and that "there is none other name under heaven given amongst men whereby they must be saved" than that of JESUS? Do you *believe* that He *alone* is "the Door of the sheep-fold;" is "the Way, the Truth, and the Life?"—that "*no man* cometh unto the Father but by Him?" If so, think of the state of these unsaved ones; and solemnly examine yourself in the sight of GOD, to see whether you are doing *your utmost* to make Him known to them.

Before proceeding further it may be well to give a Conspectus presenting at one view the whole work of the Protestant Missions in China in March, 1884.

CONSPECTUS OF PROTESTANT

PROVINCES, &c., WITHOUT RESIDENT MISSIONARIES.

KWANG-SI	... Pop.	5 mills.
HU-NAN	... Pop.	16 "
HO-NAN	... Pop.	15 "
MONGOLIA, &c...	Pop.	7 "
THIBET ...	... Pop.	8 "

							KWANG-TUNG.											FUH-KIEN.					CHEH-KIANG.							
Population in Millions / Province							17,500,000.											10,000,000.					12,000,000.							
Total No. of Missionaries / Do. Men (*m.*) and Women (*w.*)							73 / 55 *m.* 18 *w.*											46 / 37 *m.* 9 *w.*					44 / 31 *m.* 13 *w.*							
SOCIETIES, WITH DATE OF COMMENCING OPERATIONS.	*Total, including absentees.*	*Absent.*	*Total in China.*	*Married Men.*	*Single Men.*	*Single Women.*	CANTON.	Fat-shan.	HONG-KONG.	SWA-TOW.	Shiu-kwan.	Chong-lok.	Sin-on.	Li-long.	Yun-on.	Fuk-wing.	HAI-NAN.	FOO-CHOW.	Shao-wu.	AMOY.	T'AI-WAN.	TAM-SUI.	NING-PO.	Shao-hing.	Hang-chau.	Fung-hwa.	T'ai-chau.	WEN-CHOW.	Kiu-chau.	Kin-hwa.
GRAND TOTAL	480	52	428	240	85	103	25	1	17	15	2	3	3	3	2	1	1	18	1	19	6	2	17	6	11	1	1	3	4	1
BRITISH :—																														
1. London Mission, 1808	27	3	24	13	9	2	2	..	3	..	..	..	..	..	..	..	..	..	..	5	..	..	..	..	..	..	..	..	..	..
2. Bible Society, B. and F., 1843	10	1	9	3	6	..	..	..	1	..	..	..	..	..	..	..	..	..	..	1	..	..	..	..	..	..	..	..	..	..
3. " Scottish, 1868	4	1	3	1	2	..	..	..	..	..	..	..	..	..	..	..	..	..	..	..	..	..	..	..	..	..	..	..	..	..
4. Church Missionary Socy., 1844	26	3	23	18	2	3	1	..	2	..	..	..	..	..	..	..	..	8	..	..	..	..	4	3	3	..	..	..	..	..
5. " S. P. G., 1874	6	..	6	1	5	..	..	..	..	..	..	..	..	..	..	..	..	..	..	..	..	..	..	..	..	..	..	..	..	..
6. Presb. Miss., English, 1848	25	4	21	13	4	4	..	..	..	8	..	..	..	..	..	..	..	..	..	7	6	..	..	..	..	..	..	..	..	..
7. " Irish, 1869	2	..	2	1	1	..	..	..	..	..	..	..	..	..	..	..	..	..	..	..	..	..	..	..	..	..	..	..	..	..
8. " Scottish U.P., 1865	7	2	5	5	..	..	..	..	..	..	..	..	..	..	..	..	..	..	..	..	..	..	..	..	..	..	..	..	..	..
9. " Canadian, 1871	2	..	2	2	..	..	..	..	..	..	..	..	..	..	..	..	..	..	..	..	..	2	..	..	..	..	..	..	..	..
10. " Ch. of Scotland, 1878	3	1	2	2	..	..	..	..	..	..	..	..	..	..	..	..	..	..	..	..	..	..	..	..	..	..	..	..	..	..
11. Methodist, Wesleyan, 1851	16	4	12	5	7	..	2	1	..	..	2	..	..	..	..	..	..	..	..	..	..	..	..	..	..	..	..	..	..	..
12. " New Conn., 1860	5	..	5	5	..	..	..	..	..	..	..	..	..	..	..	..	..	..	..	..	..	..	..	..	..	..	..	..	..	..
13. " Free Church, 1866	4	..	4	3	..	1	..	..	..	..	..	..	..	..	..	..	..	..	..	..	..	..	3	..	1	..	..	..	..	..
14. China Inland Mission, 1854,65	90	10	80	27	24	29	..	..	..	..	..	..	..	..	..	..	..	..	..	..	..	..	..	2	..	1	1	3	4	..
15. Particular Baptist Miss., 1860	7	2	5	5	..	..	..	..	..	..	..	..	..	..	..	..	..	..	..	..	..	..	..	..	..	..	..	..	..	..
16. Female Education, 1864	2	..	2	..	..	2	..	..	1	..	..	..	..	..	..	..	..	..	..	..	..	..	1	..	..	..	..	..	..	..
Unconnected	5	..	5	2	1	2	..	..	1	..	..	..	..	..	..	..	1	..	..	..	..	..	..	..	..	..	..	..	..	..
TOTAL BRITISH	241	31	210	106	61	43	5	1	8	8	2	..	..	..	..	..	1	8	..	13	6	2	8	5	4	1	1	3	4	..
AMERICAN :—																														
1. American Board (Congl.), 1830	40	4	36	21	3	12	..	..	1	..	..	..	..	..	..	..	..	4	1	..	..	..	..	..	..	..	..	..	..	..
2. Baptist Miss. Union, N., 1834	16	1	15	8	2	5	..	..	..	7	..	..	..	..	..	..	..	..	..	..	..	..	6	1	..	..	..	..	..	1
3. " Southern, 1847	13	2	11	6	1	4	4	..	..	..	..	..	..	..	..	..	..	..	..	..	..	..	..	..	..	..	..	..	..	..
4. " 7th Day, 1847	2	..	2	1	..	1	..	..	..	..	..	..	..	..	..	..	..	..	..	..	..	..	..	..	..	..	..	..	..	..
5. Protestant Episc. Miss., 1835	13	..	13	8	1	4	..	..	..	..	..	..	..	..	..	..	..	..	..	..	..	..	..	..	..	..	..	..	..	..
6. Methodist Episc., North, 1847	35	5	30	21	1	8	..	..	..	..	..	..	..	..	..	..	..	5	..	..	..	..	..	..	..	..	..	..	..	..
7. " " South, 1848	14	..	14	8	2	4	..	..	..	..	..	..	..	..	..	..	..	..	..	..	..	..	..	..	..	..	..	..	..	..
8. Presbyterian Miss., North, 1838	53	7	46	30	6	10	11	..	..	..	..	..	..	..	..	..	..	..	..	..	..	..	3	..	2	..	..	..	..	..
9. " " South, 1867	11	1	10	5	2	3	..	..	..	..	..	..	..	..	..	..	..	..	..	..	..	..	..	..	5	..	..	..	..	..
10. " Reformed Dutch, 1858	6	..	6	4	..	2	..	..	..	..	..	..	..	..	..	..	..	..	..	6	..	..	..	..	..	..	..	..	..	..
11. Women's Union, 1859	3	..	3	..	..	3	..	..	..	..	..	..	..	..	..	..	..	..	..	..	..	..	..	..	..	..	..	..	..	..
12. Bible Society, 1876	8	..	8	4	4	..	..	..	1	..	..	..	..	..	..	..	..	1	..	..	..	..	..	..	..	..	..	..	..	..
TOTAL AMERICAN	214	20	194	116	22	56	15	..	2	7	..	..	..	..	..	..	..	10	1	6	..	..	9	1	7	..	..	..	..	1
CONTINENTAL :—																														
1. Basle Mission, 1847	14	1	13	11	2	..	..	..	2	..	..	3	3	3	2	..	..	..	..	..	..	..	..	..	..	..	..	..	..	..
2. Berlin Mission, 1831	4	..	4	4	..	..	4	..	..	..	..	..	..	..	..	..	..	..	..	..	..	..	..	..	..	..	..	..	..	..
3. " Foundling Hosp., 1850	5	..	5	1	..	4	..	..	5	..	..	..	..	..	..	..	..	..	..	..	..	..	..	..	..	..	..	..	..	..
4. Rhenish Mission, 1874	2	..	2	2	..	..	1	..	..	..	..	..	..	..	..	1	..	..	..	..	..	..	..	..	..	..	..	..	..	..
TOTAL CONTINENTAL	25	1	24	18	2	4	5	..	7	..	..	3	3	3	2	1	..	..	..	..	..	..	..	..	..	..	..	..	..	..

MISSIONS IN CHINA, MARCH, 1884.

20,000,000. KIANG-SU. 68 (53 *m.* 15 *w.*)						19,000,000. SHAN-TUNG. 46 (36 *m.* 10 *w.*)							20,000,000. CHIH-LI. 55 (38 *m.* 17 *w.*)					20,500,000. HU-PEH. 25 (24 *m.* 1 *w.*)							15 ml. KIANG-SI. 5 (5 *m.*)		9 mil. GAN-HWUY. 8 (4*m.* 4*w.*)		9 mil. SHAN-SI. 18 (14*m.* 4*w.*)		7 mil. SHEN-SI. 10 (4*m.* 6*w.*)		3 mil. KAN-SUH. 3 (2*m.* 1*w.*)	20 ml. SI-CHUEN. 13 (8*m.* 5*w.*)		5 mil. YUN-NAN. 6 (6 *m.*)			4 mil. KWEI-CHAU. 3 (3 *m.*)	8 mil. MAN-CHU-RIA. 5 (5 *m.*)
SHANG-HAI.	Su-chau.	Nan-siang.	CHIN-KIANG.	Yang-chau.	Nan-kin.	CHE-FOO.	Teng-chau.	Ts'ing-chau.	Tsi-nan.	P'ang-chia.	Wu-t'ing.	Wei-hien.	PEKIN.	TIEN-TSIN.	Kalgan.	T'ung-chau.	Pao-ting.	HAN-KOW.	Han-yang.	Wu-ch'ang.	Wu-sueh.	I-CH'ANG.	Sha-shi.	Fan-ch'eng.	KIU-KIANG.	Ta-ku-t'ang.	Gan-k'ing.	WU-HU.	T'ai-yüen.	P'ing-yang.	Han-chung.	Si-gan.	Ts'in-chau.	Chung-k'ing.	Chen-tu.	Yün-nan Fu.	Ta-li Fu.	BHAMÔ (*Burmah*)	Kwei-yang.	NEW-CHWANG.
40	10	3	8	3	4	22	10	3	2	3	3	3	29	11	7	4	4	8	2	10	1	2	1	1	4	1	7	1	15	3	8	2	3	7	6	1	4	1	3	5
2													5	3				4																						
6						1																																		
													1					1																1						
2																																								
						5							1																											
																																								2
						2																																		3
																						2																		
																		2	2	2	1																			
											3			2																										
5				3		8														3			1	1		1	7		7	3	8	2	3	2	6	1	4	1	3	
								3																					2											
						1												1											1											
15				3		17		3			3		7	5				8	2	5	1	2	1	1		1	7		10	3	8	2	3	3	6	1	4	1	3	5
										3			5	2	7	4	4												5											
1			1				5																																	
2																																								
8																				5																				
			3										9	4											4			1						4						
6	5	3																																						
2	2				4	5	5		2			3	7																											
	3		2																																					
3																																								
3			2										1																											
25	10	3	8		4	5	10		2	3		3	22	6	7	4	4			5					4			1	5					4						

The foregoing Conspectus deserves the most thoughtful consideration, for in it may be seen at a glance the population of the Provinces, the number of Missionaries in each, the Stations they occupy, and the Societies to which they belong. The date at which each Society commenced operations in China is also given, and the total number of their Missionaries. The study of these figures, in the light of the foregoing pages, will surely give emphasis to our appeal. With these facts before us, and with the command of the LORD JESUS to *go* and preach the gospel to *every* creature, each one needs to ascertain whether he has a special call to stay at home. If not, shall we disobey the SAVIOUR's plain command to *go?* If, however, we can conscientiously say that duty—not inclination, not pleasure, not business—detains us here, are we labouring in prayer for these helpless ones as we might do? Are we using our influence and means as largely as they might be to help forward their salvation? In short, are we seeking *first*, for ourselves and for them, the kingdom of GOD and His righteousness, leaving to GOD to add other blessings? Oh, let us take the time to ponder the words of the unchanging GOD—"If thou forbear to deliver them that are drawn unto death, and those that are ready to be slain; if thou sayest, Behold, we knew it not; doth not He that pondereth the heart consider it? and He that keepeth *thy* soul, doth not He know it? and shall not He render to every man according to his works?"

PROVIDENTIAL FACILITIES.

It may not be unadvisable to point out a few facts tending to shew the facilities for more extensive evangelization in China.

In the first place, the *physical conformation* of China Proper is most interesting. To the west of the 112th degree of longitude the country is mountainous, and therefore less densely populated than the more easily accessible regions on the east of that line. If we equally divide the eighteen provinces at 110° E. longitude, we shall, roughly speaking, have

From 100° to 110° E. longitude, six provinces 44 millions = $^1/_5$
From 110° to 120° „ twelve „ 183 „ = $^4/_5$

As we have such free access to the whole sea-border of China, this fact is of the deepest importance.

But further, the eastern half of China may be subdivided at 30° N. latitude into the more hilly region on the south, and the region containing greatest plains to the north, of that degree. Here, again, we find the healthier plains of the north to be far more populous than the less accessible regions of the south—regions in which the difficulty of the language is much greater,

THE WATER-WAYS OF CHINA—BOATS AND JUNKS OUTSIDE A CITY.

and the prejudice against Europeans. much stronger than in the north. Speaking generally, we may say that, subdividing the eastern half of China Proper,—

From 20° to 30° N. latitude contains ... 70½ millions
From 30° to 40° „ „ ... 112½ „

How interesting to the Christian philanthropist to find that about one-half of the population of China Proper is located in one-quarter of its territory; in that quarter, too, where access to the interior, acquisition of the spoken languages, and intercourse with the people, are beset with comparatively few difficulties.

The rivers of China give easy access to the great plains, and form, with their tributary streams, high roads into, or lead near to every province of the empire. Where water conveyance fails, wheel-barrows or carts, sedan chairs or mule litters, camels, horses, mules, or donkeys are to be hired for overland transit at fairly moderate rates. Inns are found on all high roads, and money can be easily and safely remitted to nearly every part of the empire.

In the second place, we should notice that we have now by treaty the *right of access* to every part of the empire; and that, in point of fact, there are very few places in the eighteen provinces, or in the Northern Dependencies to which access is denied us. We have not obtained settlements in all parts of the land, but in a few cities only is an itinerant visit impracticable. On this point a reference to the maps shewing the itinerations of the members of the C.I.M. is conclusive.

In the third place, we must not overlook the effect of the recent *rebellions, famines*, &c., in shaking the confidence of many of the people in their gods of wood and stone, and in preparing them to feel their need of something better, on which they may really rest. These providences seemed dark and mysterious; but the LORD was at work. The rough plough of war, famine, and pestilence, was breaking up the soil and opening it; and many a homestead, many a nest did it tear to pieces in its onward progress. Houses were burnt down, crops were pillaged, property was destroyed. Too often was the husband left a widower, or the wife a widow; parents were left childless, children were bereft of their parents. And now shall we be idle, and allow our opportunity to be lost? Missionaries tell us of such willingness to hear the gospel as never was found before. There are, indeed, opened hearts just needing the balm of Gilead and the GOOD PHYSICIAN. Shall we not send to them the precious invitation, "Come unto ME, all ye that labour and are heavy-laden, and I will give you rest?"

Lastly. The *nature of the languages* of China affords both facilities and encouragement for missionary effort. The Mandarin dialect prevails with more or less purity over the districts occupied by fully three-fourths of the people. By the translations of the Word of GOD, and of numerous tracts and books into the written language (which is current throughout the whole of the country), and into the Mandarin (which is easily read except in FUH-KIEN and KWANG-TUNG and perhaps a small part of KWANG-SI), a way has been prepared for usefulness among the literary classes of every part of the Chinese empire. And dictionaries, vocabularies, and grammars, already exist, and prepare the way for the further study of this written language.

But still more important is the fact, that the *spoken* languages in many parts of China are so easy of acquisition that now missionaries of moderate ability may begin to use the vernacular of almost any part of China after a few months' study. Hence, while there is ample room for those whom GOD has endowed with special philological talent, there is no reason why men "full of faith and of the HOLY GHOST," who have enjoyed but few educational advantages, should not be engaged in the blessed work of carrying the gospel into the regions hitherto unevangelized. The masses of the people are unable to read or write; consequently, persons possessing only a limited education are competent to act as their teachers. By means of an adaptation of our Roman alphabet, the various spoken languages of China may be reduced to writing, and uneducated Chinese may be taught to read in their own mother tongue (which the written style is *not*) in a few months. High-style composition in the unspoken written character is, even to the learned, unintelligible when read aloud: it is addressed to the eye, not to the ear. To acquire the power of using it requires, even in the case of a Chinese, several years of incessant study: hence the small proportion of the population that is able to read. Their own vernacular, all, of course, *speak;* and by means of an alphabetized system, the unlearned may be taught to *read* it in a few months. In the writer's experience in Ningpo, about three months have usually sufficed for those who were engaged in daily labour, but who regularly attended an evening class. Boys in school, able to give up more time to it, often read nicely in about a month. He has known an intelligent woman learn to read in eight or ten days sufficiently well to spell her way through any part of the New Testament. She was soon removed by friends hostile to the gospel to a distance; and her Testament and Hymn-book,* which she had during a short

* We give two verses of the hymn, "There is a fountain filled with blood," from this hymn-book.

1. Z yiu ih dzi tsi-mun-leh hyüih,
Liu-c'ih dzong Yiæ-su sing;
Væn-nying læ keh-go dzi hao gyiang.
Ze-ky'in tsih-le ken-zing.

2. Ting jih-z-kô kw'a si dao-zeh,
K'en-kyin keh dzi hwun-hyi;
Ngô ze se-tsih ziang gyi ka djong,
Yia k'o-yi gyiang-leh-kyi.

visit to the missionary's house learned to read, were through years of persecution her only comfort and help. May God hasten the time when native Christians of every part of China shall, by means of some system, like that used in Ningpo, be able to read "in their own tongue wherein they were born," that Word of God which is "profitable for doctrine, for reproof, for correction, for instruction in righteousness, that the man of God may be *perfect*, throughly furnished unto all good works."

We have now presented a brief and cursory view of the state and claims of China. To have entered into them at all in detail would have required for each province more time and space than we have devoted to the consideration of the whole empire. We have shewn how God has blest the efforts which have been put forth; and have endeavoured to lay before you the facilities which at present exist for the more extensive evangelization of this country. We have sought to press the great command of our risen Saviour, "Go ye, into all the world, and preach the gospel to every creature:" and would point out that in the parable of our Lord, contained in Matt. xxv., it was not a *stranger*, but a *servant;* not an *immoral*, but an *unprofitable* one, who was to be cast into outer darkness, where there is weeping and gnashing of teeth. "If ye love me," said our Master, "keep my commandments;" and one of these was, "Freely ye have received, freely give." We have shewn that in seven provinces of China Proper, after allowing far more than they can possibly accomplish to the Protestant missionaries and their native assistants, there still remains an overwhelming multitude altogether beyond the sound of the gospel. We have further shewn that there are eleven other provinces in China Proper still more needy,—eleven provinces, the very smallest of which exceeds Burmah in population, and which average each the population of both Scotland and Ireland combined! And what shall we say of the vast regions of Tartary and Thibet,—more extensive than the whole continent of Europe, all without any Protestant missionary save the four in New-chwang? The claims of an empire like this should surely be not only admitted, but realised! Shall not the eternal interests of one-fifth of our race stir up the deepest sympathies of our nature, the most strenuous efforts of our blood-bought powers? Shall not the low wail of helpless, hopeless misery, arising from one-half of the heathen world, pierce our sluggish ear, and rouse us, spirit, soul, and body, to one mighty, continued, unconquerable effort for China's salvation? that, strong in God's strength, and in the power of His might, we may snatch the prey from the hand of the mighty, may pluck these brands from the everlasting burnings, and rescue these captives from the thraldom of sin and Satan, to grace the triumphs of our sovereign King, and to shine for ever as stars in His diadem!

We cannot but believe that the contemplation of these solemn facts has awakened in many the heartfelt prayer, "LORD, what wilt thou have *me* to do, that Thy name may be hallowed, Thy kingdom come, and Thy will be done in China?" It is the prayerful consideration of these facts, and the deepening realisation of China's awful destitution of all that can make man truly happy, that constrains the writer to lay its claims as a heavy burden upon the hearts of those who have experienced the power of the blood of CHRIST; and to seek, first from the LORD, and then from His people, the men and the means to carry the gospel into every part of this benighted land. We have to do with Him who is the LORD of all power and might, whose arm is not shortened, whose ear is not heavy; with Him whose unchanging word directs us to ask and receive, that our joy may be full; to open our mouths wide, that He may fill them. And we do well to remember that this gracious GOD, who has condescended to place His almighty power at the command of believing prayer, looks not lightly upon the blood-guiltiness of those who neglect to avail themselves of it for the benefit of the perishing; for He it is who has said, "If thou forbear to deliver them that are drawn unto death, and those that are ready to be slain; if thou sayest, Behold, we knew it not; doth not He that pondereth the heart consider it? and He that keepeth *thy* soul, doth not He know it? and shall not He render to every man according to his works?"

THROUGH midnight gloom from Macedon,
The cry of myriads as of one;
The voiceful silence of despair
Is eloquent in awful prayer:
The soul's exceeding bitter cry,
"Come o'er and help us, or we die."

How mournfully it echoes on,
For half the earth is Macedon;
These brethren to their brethren call,
And by the LOVE which loves them all,
And by the whole world's LIFE they cry,
"O ye that live, behold we die!"

By other sounds the world is won
Than that which wails from Macedon;
The roar of gain is round it rolled,
Or men unto themselves are sold,
And cannot list the alien cry,
"O hear and help us, lest we die!"

Yet with that cry from Macedon
The very car of CHRIST rolls on:
"I come; who would abide MY day,
In yonder wilds prepare MY way;
MY voice is crying in their cry,
Help ye the dying, lest ye die."

JESU, for men of Man the SON,
Yea, THINE the cry from Macedon;
Oh, by the kingdom and the power
And glory of THINE advent hour,
Wake heart and will to hear their cry;
Help us to help them, lest we die.—(ANON.)

Such considerations as the foregoing caused the writer in 1865, so to feel the overwhelming necessity for an increase in the number of labourers in China, that, as stated in the first edition of this appeal, he did not hesitate to ask the great Lord of the harvest to call forth, to *thrust* forth, twenty-four European, and twenty-four native evangelists, to plant the standard of the cross in all the unevangelized districts of China Proper and of Chinese Tartary.

The same considerations lead us to-day to cry to God for many more. Those who have never been called to prove the faithfulness of the covenant-keeping God, in supplying, in answer to prayer, the pecuniary need of His servants, might deem it a hazardous experiment to send evangelists to a distant heathen land, with "*only* God to look to." But in one whose privilege it has been for many years past to prove the faithfulness of God, in various circumstances—at home and abroad, by land and by sea, in sickness and in health, in necessities, in dangers, and at the gates of death,—such apprehensions would be wholly inexcusable. The writer has seen God, in answer to prayer, quell the raging of the storm, alter the direction of the wind, and give rain in the midst of prolonged drought. He has seen Him, in answer to prayer, stay the angry passions and murderous intentions of violent men, and bring the machinations of His people's foes to nought. He has seen Him, in answer to prayer, raise the dying from the bed of death, when human aid was vain; has seen Him preserve from the pestilence that walketh in darkness, and from the destruction that wasteth at noonday. For more than twenty-seven years he has proved the faithfulness of God in supplying the pecuniary means for his own temporal wants, and for the need of the work he has been engaged in. He has seen God, in answer to prayer, raising up labourers not a few for this vast mission-field; supplying the means requisite for their outfit, passage, and support; and vouchsafing blessing on the efforts of many of them, both among the native Christians and the heathen Chinese in fourteen out of the eighteen provinces referred to.

For the glory of God and the refreshment of His people, he would mention more particularly some of the answers to prayer which encouraged him to form the China Inland Mission nineteen years ago.

About the latter part of 1857, the dispute between the British and Chinese authorities about the notorious lorcha *Arrow*, ended in the bombardment of Canton. This act greatly intensified the long-cherished hatred of the Cantonese towards the foreign residents in China. In Ningpo they plotted the destruction of all the foreigners; and knowing that many of them met for worship on Sunday evenings at the house of one of the missionaries, when they were always unarmed, they determined to surround the house on one of these occasions, and destroy all those assembled,—cutting off afterwards any individuals who might not have been present. They obtained the sanction of the Tao-tai, the chief civil magistrate of the place, to this plot; which might have been carried out—as was a similar one against the Portuguese a few months afterwards;—but a native, who was acquainted with the design, had a friend in the service of one of the missionaries; he warned this friend of the coming danger, and urged his leaving foreign employ. The servant made the matter known to his master, and thus the missionaries were apprised of their danger. They determined to meet together at the house of one of their number to seek the protection of the MOST HIGH, and to hide under the shadow of His wings. Nor did they thus meet in vain.

At the very time that they were praying, the LORD was working. He led an inferior mandarin,—the superintendent of customs,—to call on the Tao-tai and remonstrate with him on the folly of permitting such an attempt; which, he assured him, would rouse the foreigners in other parts to come with armed forces to avenge the death of their countrymen, and raze the city to the ground. The Tao-tai replied, that when the foreigners came for that purpose, he should deny all knowledge of, or complicity in, the plot; and so turn their vengeance against the Cantonese, who would, in their turn, be destroyed; "and thus," said he, "we shall get rid of Cantonese and foreigners by one stroke of policy." The superintendent of customs assured him that all such attempts at evasion would be useless; and, finally, the Tao-tai sent to the Cantonese, withdrawing his permission, and prohibiting the attack. This took place at the very time when we were asking protection of the LORD; though we did not become acquainted with the facts until some weeks had elapsed. Thus we proved that

"Sufficient was His arm alone,
And our defence was sure."

And not only have we in this, and in many other circumstances of external danger, found Him "a very present help in trouble;" we have likewise experienced His faithfulness in supplying our temporal wants, in answer to prayer. A few instances may be referred to. In the latter part of the year 1857, having been nursing a missionary brother who died of small-pox,* it was necessary to lay aside the clothing which had been worn in attendance on him, for fear of conveying the contagion to others. Being at this time in possession of less money than was requisite to procure what was needed, prayer was the only resource. The LORD answered it by the unexpected arrival of a box of clothing left some months before in Swatow, in the south of China.

* The Rev. J. W. Quarterman, of the American Presbyterian Mission North.

About two months later, under date of November 18th, 1857, the following was penned:—

"Many think I am very poor. This certainly is true enough in one sense; but, thank GOD, it is 'poor and making many rich; having nothing, yet possessing all things.' And 'my GOD will supply *all* my need:' to Him be all the glory. I would not be otherwise than as I am, dependent myself on the LORD, and used as a means of helping others. The mail arrived on the 4th, Saturday. That morning, as usual, we supplied a breakfast to the destitute who came for it. There were seventy in number; sometimes they do not reach forty, at others they exceed eighty. They come every day, Lord's day excepted; as then we cannot get through our other duties, and attend to them too. Well; we paid all expenses, and provided for ourselves for the morrow; after which we (Mr. Jones and myself) had not a dollar left. We knew not *how* the LORD would provide for Monday; but over our mantel-piece are two rolls in the Chinese character, 'Ebenezer' (Hitherto hath the LORD helped us), and 'Jehovah Jireh' (The LORD will provide); and He gave us not to doubt for a moment. The mail came in a week sooner than was expected, and Mr. Jones received a bill for 214 dols. We thanked GOD and took courage, went to a merchant's, and though there is usually some days' delay ere we get the money, this time he said, 'Send down on Monday.' We sent, and though he had not been able to buy all the dollars, he sent seventy on account, so all was well. * * * * Oh! it is sweet thus to live *directly* dependent on the LORD, *who never fails us*. On Monday the poor had their breakfast as usual, for we had not told them not to come, being assured that it was the LORD's work, and 'Jehovah Jireh.' We could not help our eyes filling with tears of gratitude, when we saw not only ourselves supplied, but the widows and orphans, the blind and the lame, the friendless and the destitute, together provided for, by the bounty of Him who feeds the ravens. 'O magnify the LORD with me, and let us exalt His name together.' 'O taste and see that the LORD is good; blessed is the man that trusteth in *Him*. O fear the LORD, ye His saints; for there is no want to them that fear Him. The young lions *do* lack and suffer hunger; but they that seek the LORD shall not lack *any good thing*.' (And if *not* good, why want anything?) 'None of them that trust in *Him* shall be desolate.'"

When the pecuniary supplies mentioned in the above extract were exhausted, and only one solitary cash (the twentieth part of a penny) now remained in the possession of the writer and his colleague, Mr. Jones, GOD again manifested His providential care. There remained on the 6th of January, 1858, sufficient food in the house to furnish a scanty breakfast. That partaken of, having neither food for the rest of the day, nor money to purchase it, we could only cry, "Give us *this day* our daily bread."

After prayer and deliberation, we thought that perhaps we ought to attempt to dispose of something we possessed, in order to supply our immediate need. But on looking round we saw nothing that we could well spare, and little that the Chinese would purchase for ready money. Credit to any extent we might have had, could we have conscientiously availed ourselves of it; but this we felt to be unscriptural in itself, as well as inconsistent with the position we were in,—namely, that of serving GOD, and subsisting on what He Himself had given us, or might from time to time supply. We had indeed one article which we knew the Chinese would readily purchase,—an iron stove;

but we could not but regret the necessity for parting with it. We set out, however, to the founder's, and after a walk of some length came to the river, which we had intended to cross by a floating bridge of boats; but here the LORD shut up our path. The bridge of boats had been carried away during the preceding night, and the river could only be crossed by a ferry, the fare of which was two cash each person. As we only possessed one between us, our course clearly was to return and await GOD's own interposition on our behalf.

When we reached home, we found that Mrs. Jones had gone with her children to dine with a friend, in accordance with an invitation accepted some days previously. Mr. Jones, though himself included in the invitation, refused now to go and leave me to fast alone. We carefully searched our cupboards, and though there was nothing to eat, we found a small packet of cocoa. This, with a little hot water, somewhat revived us; and again we cried to the LORD, and "the LORD heard, and saved us out of all our troubles." While still on our knees, a letter arrived containing a remittance from England. And this timely supply not only met the immediate and urgent need of the day: in the assured confidence that that GOD, whose we were and whom we served, would not put to shame those whose whole and only trust was in Himself, the writer's marriage had been previously arranged to take place just fourteen days after this date; and this expectation was not disappointed; for the mountains shall depart, and the hills be removed, but His kindness shall not depart from His people, neither shall His covenant fail. And though during subsequent years our faith has often been exercised, and sometimes severely, He has ever proved faithful to His promise, and has not suffered us to lack any good thing.

A somewhat different though not less manifest answer to prayer was vouchsafed early in the year 1859. The dear wife of the writer was brought very low by illness, and all hope of recovery was gone. Every remedy tried had proved unavailing, and her physician, Dr. William Parker, had nothing more to suggest. Life seemed fast ebbing away. The only ground of hope was that GOD might yet see fit to raise her up in answer to believing but submissive prayer. The afternoon for the usual prayer-meeting among the missionaries had arrived, and the writer sent a request for prayer, which was most warmly responded to. Just at this time, a remedy which had not been tried was suggested to the mind of the writer, and he felt that without delay he must hasten to consult with Dr. Parker as to the propriety of using it. It was a moment of anguish. The hollow temples, sunken eyes, and pinched features, denoted the near approach of death; and it seemed very questionable whether life would hold out till this could be done. It was nearly two miles to Dr. Parker's house, and every moment appeared long. On his way thither, while wrestling mightily with GOD in prayer, the precious words, "Call upon ME in the day of trouble; I will deliver thee, and thou shalt glorify Me," were brought with power to his soul. He was enabled to plead them in faith, and the result was deep, deep, unspeakable peace and joy. All consciousness of distance was gone. Dr. Parker approved of the use of the remedy suggested; but when the writer arrived at home, he saw at a glance that the desired change had already taken place, in the absence of this or any other remedy. The pinched aspect of the countenance had given place to the calm appearance of tranquil slumber, and not one unfavourable symptom recurred to retard recovery to health and strength.

SUPPORT FOR THE NINGPO HOSPITAL.

In the autumn of the same year, Dr. Parker was suddenly compelled to return to Glasgow, with his motherless children, Mrs. Parker having died of cholera. He requested the writer to take charge of the missionary hospital at Ningpo, which must otherwise be closed.

After a few days of earnest prayer for Divine guidance, the writer felt constrained to undertake it, relying on a prayer-answering GOD to furnish the means requisite for its support. The funds for its maintenance had been hitherto supplied by the proceeds of the doctor's foreign medical practice: with his departure these ceased. But had not GOD said, that whatever we ask in the name of the LORD JESUS shall be done unto us? and are we not told to seek *first* the kingdom of GOD—not means to advance it—and *all these things* shall be added to us? Such promises were surely sufficient.

Eight days previous to entering upon this responsibility, the writer had not the most remote idea of doing so. Still less could friends at home have anticipated it. But the LORD had foreseen the need, and already funds were on their way to supply it. At times there were not less than fifty in-patients in the hospital, besides a large number who daily attended as out-patients. Thirty beds were ordinarily allotted to free patients and their attendants, and about as many to opium smokers, who paid for their board while being cured of their habit. As all the wants of the sick in the hospital were supplied gratuitously, as were likewise the remedial appliances needed by the out-patients, the daily expense was considerable; besides which a number of native attendants were required, involving their support. But from the very first the LORD provided all that was requisite for the support of the institution, in addition to what was needed for the maintenance of the writer and his family, and the carrying on of the other branches of missionary work under his superintendence. And when, nine months later, he was compelled through failure of health to relinquish this charge, he was able to leave more funds for the support of the sick than were placed in his hands at the time he undertook it.

But not only were pecuniary supplies vouchsafed in answer to prayer. Many lives were spared; persons apparently in hopeless stages of disease were restored; and success was given in cases of serious and dangerous operations. In the case of one poor man, both of whose legs were amputated under very unfavourable circumstances, healthy action took place with such rapidity, that both wounds were healed in less than two weeks. And more permanent benefits than these were conferred. Many were convinced of the truth of Christianity; not a few sought the Lord by prayer, and experienced the power of the Good Physician to cure the sin-sick soul. During the nine months above alluded to, sixteen patients from the hospital were baptized, and more than thirty others became candidates for admission into one or other of the mission churches in Ningpo.

FUNDS FOR RETURN TO ENGLAND.

The incessant physical and mental labour inseparable from the sole charge of such an institution, in addition to the other missionary duties still devolving on the writer, produced an effect which, though anticipated, could not in the absence of additional labourers be avoided; but which afforded another occasion for the manifestation of the faithfulness and loving care of Him, who works all things after the counsel of His own will. Completely prostrated by repeated attacks of illness, the only hope of restoration to health seemed to be in a voyage to England, and a temporary residence in his native land. As heretofore, God was present with His aid. The means for return were supplied; and that so liberally, that we were able to bring with us a native Christian to assist in translations or revisions, and to instruct in the language such helpers as the Lord might raise up for the carrying on and extension of the work. That He would do this we had no doubt, as we had been enabled to seek it from Him in earnest, believing prayer for many months previously. Under date of January 16th, 1860, we had written to a Christian friend in England as follows:—

"Do you know of any earnest, devoted young men, desirous of serving God in China; who, *not wishing for more than their expenses*, would be willing to come out and labour here? Oh, for *four* or *five* such helpers! They would probably preach in Chinese in six months. In answer to prayer the means would be found."

The day before leaving China, we wrote as follows to our friend, W. T.

Berger, Esq., whom we had known before leaving England, and who had ever strengthened our hands in the LORD while in that distant land :—

"We are bringing a young Chinese brother with us to assist in translating, and, I hope, to assist in teaching the dialect to fellow-labourers, if the LORD induce any to return with us."

And throughout our voyage our earnest prayer to GOD was that He would overrule our return for good to China, and make it instrumental in raising up *at least five helpers* to labour in Ningpo and the province of CHEH-KIANG.

PRAYER FOR WORKERS FOR CHEH-KIANG.

We had not been long in England ere we met with some Christian brothers desirous of serving GOD in China. We had more or less intercourse, both personally and by correspondence, with five; and after much prayer were led to invite one of them, Mr. James Meadows, to London, to reside with us for a time; with a view to our making his acquaintance more perfectly, and to his commencing the study of the language. He made such progress as left no doubt of his ability to master the language; and the health of Mr. Jones at Ningpo failing rapidly, we were enabled, through the co-operation and aid of our kind friend, Mr. Berger, to take a passage for Mr. Meadows and his young wife in the *Challenger* in January, 1862. He arrived in Ningpo in the month of June, and was soon able to commence missionary work. In the temporary absence of Mr. Jones in the month of September, and before Mr. Meadows was able to speak and preach with fluency, he conducted the meetings by giving out hymns and reading portions of Scripture in the colloquial; while the native helpers would give an address or exhortation, and engage in prayer. In two months from this time he opened a day-school for native boys, with the aid of a Chinese teacher; and when Mr. Jones left China, his presence there became invaluable.

Mr. Meadows found his work at first far from easy. Besides the difficulties arising from his, as yet, imperfect knowledge of the language, the state of society was only slowly recovering from the violent upheaving to which it had been subjected by the rebels, and the converts were still very much scattered. But by GOD's grace, our good brother persevered, and success crowned his efforts. Some who had been under discipline were restored; others who had been cold and dead were quickened. The services of the native brother first given to us were blessed. A simple countryman, converted six or seven years before, so fully preached the gospel in his own neighbourhood, that in going through it for ten or twelve miles round, Mr. Meadows scarcely met with an individual who had not heard more or less of the LORD JESUS from his

BUDDHIST PRIESTS PLAYING AT CHESS.

lips For in season and out of season CHRIST was and CHRIST still is his theme. Another of the members went into a Buddhist nunnery, and preached the gospel with such power, that the abbess, one of the nuns, and a neophyte about to take the veil, were converted, and added to the church.

About this time Mrs. Lord, who conducted an orphan school in faith in the living GOD for supplies, had likewise been much blessed in labouring amongst the native women, to whom GOD gave her a wide door of access. She had one or two Chinese Christians with her, labouring as Bible-women.

Writing in 1864, she stated that if she had five Bible-women, she could give to each of them districts which would find them ample employment; and that she might herself be employed from morning to night, in teaching Chinese women to read the Scriptures in the Romanized colloquial. With the duties of the orphan school devolving upon her, this was, of course, impossible: and as opportunities for working among the women continually increased, she wrote most earnestly, begging for some one to be sent out to assist her in the orphan school.

NINGPO WOMAN.

It was distressing to hear of large districts where every house was open, whose female residents were eager to hear her instruction,—districts, in each of which she might have spent the whole of every day, but to which she could only devote a few hours weekly or fortnightly, on account of other claims, equally or still more imperative. As the orphan work was carried on in faith, it was necessary that any one assisting in it should be able to depend upon GOD for personal support. Much earnest prayer was offered that GOD would raise up a suitable helper. *We* knew of none; but at a meeting for prayer of the members of the committee of the Foreign

Evangelist Society, the writer was led to lay before them, as a subject for intercession, Mrs. Lord's need of a female helper; and to read to them an extract from one of her letters.

A Second Worker.

The secretary, Mr. George Pearce, immediately replied, that it was very remarkable that he had just received a letter speaking of one who seemed in every way suited for the proposed work. We made her acquaintance; the Foreign Evangelist Society kindly provided the expense of her passage to China, and other friends contributed the requisite funds for her outfit. She arrived in Ningpo about the middle of February, 1865. Mrs. Lord wrote, on April 5th, that she was already able to help her a great deal in the school, in which she continued to work until her marriage.

A Third Worker.

On the 25th of September, 1863, Mr. Barchet called on the writer and signified his desire to preach CHRIST to the poor Chinese. A native of Stuttgart in Germany, he came to England in 1861, desiring to escape the restraint of his father's roof, and to enjoy the world. At the house of a friend, he met Mr. Hall, a deacon of the church of which he subsequently became a member, who lent him a copy of "The LORD's Dealings with George Müller." At this time, Mr. Günzler, a German curate, and a very dear friend of Mr. Barchet, came to London to preach during the time of the Exhibition of 1862; and Mr. Barchet rejoiced to meet his friend once more. After being absent from home for a few days, on his return he hastened to visit Mr. Günzler again; but found him lying dead, having been suddenly carried off by typhus fever. He went home, crushed with sorrow, and asking himself, "Where should I be if I died so?" He prayed, read the Scriptures, and also the account of the conversion of Mr. George Müller (of Bristol) in the book that had been lent him, and argued thus with himself: "Mr. Müller was a wicked young man—JESUS CHRIST pardoned him—He can pardon me—the blood that cleansed him can cleanse me." He soon afterwards found assured rest in CHRIST.

Panting now to serve his loving REDEEMER with all his powers, he offered himself, as has been stated above, for the LORD's work in China. Shortly afterwards he commenced the study of Chinese, and made remarkable progress in it. After two lessons in the language, and private study in the meantime, he wrote a note to the Chinese brother (mentioned above as having come to England), which, though far from being perfect in idiom, was still intelligible, and very creditable to one who had commenced the study but a fortnight before.

He now commenced to study medicine at the London Hospital, and in this his progress was very encouraging. He was preparing for the matriculation examination of the London University, when, very unexpectedly, the LORD opened the way for his departure to China. A gentleman residing in Scotland, a perfect stranger, most kindly offered, through Dr. Nevius, now of Chefoo, a free passage for two missionaries, in a magnificent iron steamer of which he was the owner. When this intelligence was first communicated to Mr. Barchet, and he was asked whether he was prepared to leave on so short a notice as the early departure of the steamer allowed, he spent a few moments in silent prayer, and then replied, that it would be a disappointment to go before passing the examination, for which he had been preparing for some time, and that he had hoped for much happy intercourse with the writer and his family on the voyage out; but that he was quite prepared to give these up, and to leave that very night, if it were the LORD's will.

Our brother went forth in faith in GOD, looking to Him for the supply of all his need; but the church of which he was a member determined that, as far as in them lay, it should be their privilege to supply that need, and they lovingly provided him with a suitable outfit.

His pastor wrote of him:—

"Though slightly built, he is yet capable of great exertion, very energetic, and industrious; he has a most gentle and affectionate disposition, attracting the love of all who know him; and yet he is resolute and firm. Though quite young he already writes five languages."

After experiencing much Christian hospitality and kindness in the city of Glasgow, Mr. Barchet, and another brother who had been studying Chinese for some months, sailed from the Clyde on the 1st of April. The expense of the outfit, &c., of Mr. Barchet's companion was met by unsolicited donations, sent in answer to prayer. After our friends had sailed, a Christian lady kindly sent us a donation of £30. To us there seemed no immediate need for the whole of this sum; but our FATHER had foreseen, and was providing for, an emergency which soon arose. Part of it, with other funds remaining in hand, was sent to China; and the rest was soon wanted, as will be seen from the sequel.

A Fourth Worker.

We had at this time residing with us Mr. George Crombie, from Aberdeen. He and Miss Skinner, his intended wife, were pursuing the study of the language, preparatory to missionary labour in China. Devotedly attached to each other, they had been engaged for four years or more, and were to have been married in about five or six weeks; preparations for their union being far advanced. But their departure for China was not immediately anticipated.

The steamer *Corea*, in which Mr. Barchet and his companion had sailed, proceeded as far as the south of the Bay of Biscay, when she fell in with a ship containing a valuable cargo, which had been abandoned by its crew in a severe storm. The captain took possession of this prize, worth some thousands of pounds, which thus became the property of the owner and crew of the *Corea*, and turning back, towed it into Plymouth harbour. The steamer was detained there for a few days, when the Lord permitted our faith to be severely exercised by a heavy trial. Mr. Marshall and the writer, having proceeded to Plymouth, received the painful intelligence that Mr. Barchet's companion had determined not to go forward to China. He had caught a serious cold before leaving Glasgow, had suffered much from sea-sickness, and was very ill when they reached Plymouth. Unnerved in mind and body, he felt unprepared to set out again for China.

Many circumstances combined to make the drawing back of our brother peculiarly painful to us. After many months' study, he had attained to considerable proficiency in the language. China's need we felt to be very great—"the harvest was plenteous, but the labourers were few." The free passage, so generously accorded, appeared lost; as did all immediate use of the articles procured at considerable cost for his outfit. And above all, we feared disgrace to the cause of our God, and discouragement to the friends of the mission work. At this critical juncture, our beloved brother, Mr. Crombie, nobly stepped forward to fill up the gap; and this, not only with the assent of his intended bride, but with her hearty concurrence. "Go!" she said, "and shew that you love the cause of God more than me." After two hours of prayerful consideration, he calmly resolved to make the sacrifice; and proceeded to Plymouth by the first express train of the next morning. In sixteen hours after the receipt of the telegram announcing the drawing back of Mr. Barchet's companion, Mr. Crombie was on his way to take his place, provided the consent of the captain and the owner of the vessel could be obtained. He arrived in Plymouth about 4.45 p.m. The captain's consent had in the meantime been conditionally given, and the owner's kind permission reached us about an hour after Mr. Crombie's arrival. A few necessary articles were hastily purchased; we saw our dear brother on board, united in prayer with him and Mr. Barchet, and about half an hour after midnight left them already on their way to China.

They were favoured with a prosperous passage as far as the Cape of Good Hope. They put into Table Bay for the purpose of taking in coal; but not finding any there, the captain decided on Tuesday evening, May 16th, to take the steamer into Simon's Bay. As they left Table Bay they had very rough weather, but through the goodness of God were preserved from every danger. The gale which was commencing in the evening as they left, increased in violence through the night, and raged the next day with terrific fury. At 10 a.m. on Wednesday, there were twenty-eight sea-going vessels and about thirty smaller craft in Table Bay. By 8 p.m., eighteen of the sea-going vessels and all the smaller craft were stranded or destroyed. The following extracts from the "*Port Louis Commercial Gazette*" of June 10th, 1865, are given to shew how great was the danger, and how real and remarkable was the deliverance which our dear brothers experienced.

"Cape Town, *Friday, May 19th*, 1865.

"One of the most destructive gales that have ever visited Table Bay occurred on Wednesday, the 17th inst., two days after the departure of the mail steamer *Roman* for England.

"We are obliged to pass over the description of the wrecks as they occurred [during the day], and the efforts made to save lives and property, and come to the more important part of the narrative.

"At this time (sunset) the scene was terrible in the extreme. Immediately before he finally sank behind the Lion's Hill, the sun broke through the barrier of clouds that had intercepted his rays during the day, and shone brightly upon the Bay, illuminating for the moment every feature of the scene of havoc. At this time there were lying upon the beach, more or less dismantled, fifteen sea-going vessels, besides smaller craft; a tremendous sea was rolling in, threatening every moment to carry away the few vessels remaining at their anchors. The barque *City of Peterborough*, and the steamer *Dane* were dragging their anchors, and signalling in vain for more anchors and warps. The steamer *Athens* also was shewing signals of distress, and letting off large quantities of steam, shewing that she was prepared at any moment to put forth her full power. There was every prospect of the gale increasing, with a probability that ere the morning should break, there would not be a vessel remaining at anchor. Mr. Anderson offered £500 for an anchor to be run to the *Dane*, and Mr. Searle £1000 for one for the *City of Peterborough*; but without effect; no boat would incur the risk. Directly afterwards, the *Athens* signalled that her last anchor was gone; and on such a scene the sun went down.

"After the sun had set, the fury of the gale increased. The barometer continued to fall. The *City of Peterborough* had been dragging her anchors all day. Shortly after sunset she broke adrift, and finally struck upon a reef some distance from the shore. The cries of her crew for assistance could be plainly heard from the shore, but all attempts to communicate with them failed. The captain (Wright), his wife and child, and a crew of fifteen, all perished.

"But the most shocking catastrophe was the loss of the mail steamer *Athens*. About six o'clock in the evening her last anchor parted, and she attempted to steam out to sea. At first she appeared to make considerable headway; but before seven o'clock she drifted broadside on to the rocks near Green Point, and very speedily broke up. The calls for help of those on board of her could be distinctly heard upon the shore amid the roar of the breakers; but the crowd of persons whom these cries attracted were powerless to aid. All that those on shore could do was to light a fire, and thereby indicate to those on board that their peril was known. There was not a rope or lantern at the lighthouse; no rockets nor Manby apparatus within a mile or two of the spot. And yet for two hours a continued wail of anguish and appeals for help came from the steamer, which occasionally could be seen lying on the rocks; she was broken-backed, but still above water, with masts standing, till after nine o'clock. Fragments of wreck washing ashore then bore testimony that the ship was rapidly breaking up. About ten o'clock the cries ceased, and thick darkness gathered over the scene. Captain Smith, Dr. Curtis, and all hands perished. There were thirty persons on board of her. She was to have left for Mauritius on the following day, but fortunately none of her passengers had embarked.

"Of twenty-eight sea-going vessels in the Bay at 10 a.m. on Wednesday, at 8 p.m. on the same day but ten remained. In Simon's Bay also the gale was very severely felt."

During this dreadful day eighty or ninety lives were lost in Table Bay; but our friends were preserved in Simon's Bay from all harm. Not in vain had the prayers of many of GOD's people been offered for their preservation;—they were not unneeded,—they were not unanswered.

On the following Lord's-day our friends went ashore, and were most kindly received and entertained by one of the missionaries of Simon's Town. They had an opportunity of preaching; and after the evening service, a lady asked their acceptance of a purse containing £4. They were both refreshed and encouraged by this token of Christian love; but they did not know how seasonable the help would prove to be when they reached Hong-kong, at which port they safely arrived in due course. One of their first enquiries was for letters, but to their disappointment they found none. Letters (some of which contained remittances) had been sent to them by different individuals, and by two or three successive mails; but, strange to say, not one of them was then forthcoming, though all were ultimately received. All the money they had was consequently needed, and proved just sufficient to pay their passage by a Hamburg barque which was going direct to Ningpo. They arrived there on the 24th of July, and found other letters and remittances awaiting them. Thus ended a voyage remarkable from first to last for providential mercies.

The Fifth Worker.

We must now take our readers back to the day when our two brothers sailed from Plymouth. In his own cabin on board the *Corea*, on the 12th of April, Mr. Crombie requested the writer to hasten the departure of Miss Skinner as much as possible, that the painful separation might not be needlessly prolonged. He was assured that no effort on the writer's part should be wanting; but was reminded that we had not £1 in hand towards the £75 or £80* that would probably be needed for her outfit and passage. We knelt down in his cabin and asked Him who opens and no man shuts, who shuts and no man opens, to provide the needed means and suitable escort for her going forth. Mr. Crombie writing from Teneriffe *sent no note for her, expecting*

* The expense now is much less; now we expend £55 on outfit and passage to China.

and believing this prayer to be answered. And he was not mistaken; for on the 26th of April, just one fortnight after Mr. Crombie's departure, Miss Skinner sailed for China in the *Prince Alfred*, Captain Ellison, her passage and outfit all provided by a prayer-answering GOD, through His believing people. She sailed, too, under the escort of a missionary and his wife, and in a vessel whose captain and chief officer were both Christian men. After a pleasant and useful voyage she safely reached her destination, and was in due course united in marriage to Mr. Crombie.

FORMATION OF THE CHINA INLAND MISSION.

When Miss Skinner had sailed, the prayer was fully answered which had been first offered to the LORD in China in the year 1859, for *five* additional labourers for the work in Ningpo and the province of CHEH-KIANG; and we felt in 1865, that in going forward and seeking from the LORD *twenty-four* more labourers for the interior provinces, we were not entering on a new and untried path of service. The same GOD who raised up these five workers could raise up others to follow them, and to extend the work into every province of China. We believed that He could—that He would—raise up, "willing, skilful men" for every department of service. All we proposed to do was to lay hold on His faithfulness who called us to this service; and in obedience to *His* call, and in reliance on *His* power, to enlarge the sphere of our operations, for the glory of His name who alone doeth wondrous things.

The question, however, was sometimes raised as to whether the interior of China, though evidently needing the gospel, and nominally open to us by treaty-right, would, in point of fact, prove accessible. We met this question by another:—When the LORD JESUS gives a definite command, is it our place to ask whether it can be obeyed or not? The terms of His command are explicit,—in "*all* the world" and "to *every* creature." He would have the gospel preached; and He answers every objection and meets every difficulty in the very outset, by assuring us that all power is given unto Him in heaven and in earth; and that He who is true, and therefore can neither fail nor forget—who hath the key of David, to open or to shut as pleaseth Him—is with us alway, even unto the end of the world. The dangers and difficulties in the way we knew would be neither few nor small; but with JESUS for our leader we feared not to follow on. We expected that dangers, and difficulties, and trials, while leading to a greater realisation of our own weakness, and poverty, and need, would also constrain us to lean more constantly, to draw more deeply,

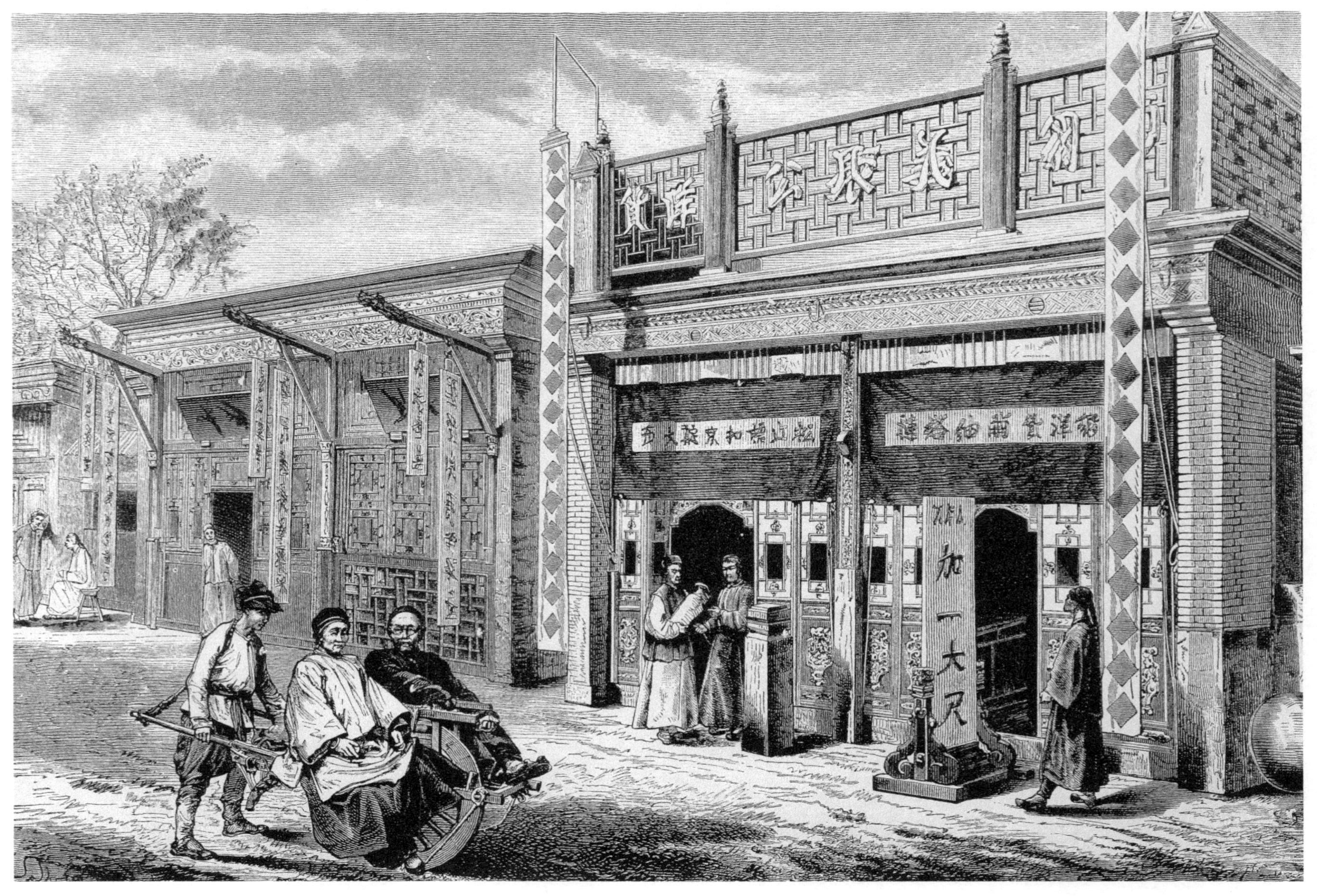

THE CHINESE WHEEL-BARROW.

and to rest more implicitly, on the strength, the riches, the fulness of CHRIST. "In the world ye shall have tribulation, but in Me ye shall have peace," we knew would be the experience of those engaged in the work. If times of the greatest trial and danger would be for GOD's glory, for the benefit of His cause, and for the true interest of those labouring, at such times either His delivering power would be shewn forth most conspicuously, or else His sustaining grace would prove sufficient for the weakest servant in the conflict. And what shall we say now, after an experience of eighteen or nineteen years in this work? Have we been disappointed in the confident xpectation of GOD's help with which we set out? Far from it! We can only say, in the words of Joshua of old, "Not one thing hath failed of all the good things which the LORD our GOD spake concerning us; all are come to pass unto us, and not one thing hath failed thereof."

Expecting this little work to fall into the hands of some who might be led to think of personally engaging in the work, the writer referred in the earlier editions to the following incidents in his own experience, in which GOD's providential interposition on behalf of His servants was very manifest. For the same reason he still retains them.

In April, 1855, the writer (in company with the Rev. J. S. Burdon of the Church Missionary Society*), visited the island of Tsung-ming and the north bank of the Yang-tse-kiang, for the purpose of preaching the gospel and of distributing copies of the New Testament. The following extracts are taken from the writer's journal at the time :—

"*Thursday, April 26th.*—Having started at daybreak, about breakfast-time we arrived at Jen-how-kiang. After breakfast, we commended ourselves to the care of our heavenly FATHER and sought His blessing before proceeding to this great city. The day was the very opposite of yesterday, being as dull and wet as that was fine and clear. We both felt persuaded that Satan would not let us assail his kingdom as we had done, without raising up opposition or persecution; but we also felt fully assured that it was the will of GOD that we should preach CHRIST here, and distribute the Word of Truth to this people. We were sorry that we had so few books left for so important a place, but the result proved that this also was providential.

"Our teachers endeavoured to persuade us not to go; but we determined, by GOD's help, that nothing should hinder us. We directed them, however, to remain in one of the boats; and, if we did not return, to learn all that they could respecting our fate, and make all possible haste to Shanghai, and give information to our friends. We also left orders that the other boat should remain a little outside, if we did not return that night; so that if we did afterwards get back, we might not be detained for want of a boat. We then put all our books, except some dozen or less, into two bags, and with one servant, who always accompanied us on these occasions, set off for the city, some twenty *li*, or seven miles, distant. Walking was out of the question, both from the state of the roads, and from the distance; so we availed ourselves of the wheel-barrow, here the

* Now the esteemed Bishop of Victoria, Hong-kong.

only conveyance to be had. It is cheaper than the sedan, only requiring one coolie; but is by no means an agreeable conveyance on rough, dirty roads.

"We had not got far before the servant requested permission to go back, as he was thoroughly frightened by the reports he heard of the native soldiers. Of course we at once consented, as we did not wish to involve any one else in trouble; determining to carry our books ourselves, and look for physical as well as spiritual strength to Him who has promised to supply *all* our need. A very respectable man came and warned us against proceeding, as we should find to our sorrow what the Tung-chow militia were, if we did. We thanked him for his advice, but did not act upon it, as our hearts were fixed; and whether to bonds, imprisonment, or death; or whether to distribute our scriptures, tracts, &c., in safety, and return unhurt, we knew not: but we determined, by the grace of God, not to leave Tung-chow without the gospel, nor its teeming thousands to die in uncared - for ignorance of the way of life. A few more steps and my wheel-barrow man would proceed no further; so I had to seek another, who was fortunately easily found.

"As we went on, the ride in the rain and through the mud was anything but agreeable. We could not help feeling our position, though we wavered not for a moment. At intervals we encouraged one another with promises of Scripture, and verses of hymns. That verse,—

The perils of the sea,
  The perils of the land,
Should not dishearten thee,
  Thy *Lord* is nigh at hand.
But should thy courage fail,
  When tried and sore oppressed,
His promise shall avail,
  And set thy soul at rest,

seemed particularly appropriate to our position, and was very comforting to me. On our way, we passed through a small town of about a thousand inhabitants, called Sing-kiau Chen; and here, in the mandarin dialect, I preached Jesus to a good number of people. I never was so happy in speaking of the love of God and of the atonement of Jesus Christ; my own soul was richly blessed, and filled with joy and peace; and I was able to speak with unusual ease and freedom. And how gladdened was my heart when, afterwards, I heard one of my hearers repeating to the new comers, in his own native dialect, the truths I had been telling him. Oh! how thankful I felt to hear a Chinese, of his own accord, telling his fellow-countrymen that God loved them; that they were sinners, but that Jesus died instead of them, and paid the penalty of their guilt. That one moment repaid me for all the trials I had passed through; and I felt that if the Lord granted His Holy Spirit to change the heart of that man, we had not come here in vain: I felt as if I could say with Simeon, 'Lord, now lettest Thou Thy servant depart in peace.' We distributed a few Testaments and tracts, for the people read well, and we could not leave them without the gospel. It was well we did so, for when we reached Tung-chow, we found we had quite as many left as we had strength to carry.

"Passing on, as we approached the western suburb of the city, the prayer of the early Christians (Acts iv. 24—29) when persecution was commencing, came to my mind; and in the petition, 'And now, Lord, behold their threatenings, and grant unto thy servants, that with all boldness they may speak thy word,' I most heartily joined. Before entering the suburb, we laid our plans, so that we might act in concert; and told our wheel-barrow men where to await us, that they might not be involved in any trouble on our account. Then, looking up to our heavenly Father, we committed ourselves to His keeping, took our bags, and set off for the city.

"We walked along the principal street leading to the west gate, for some time uninterfered with; and were a little amused at the unusual title of Huh-kway-tsz (black devils), which was applied to us. We wondered at it at the time, but afterwards found it was our clothes, and not our skin, that gave origin to it. As we passed several of the soldiers, I remarked to Mr. Burdon that these were the men we had heard so much of, and yet they seemed inclined to let us pass

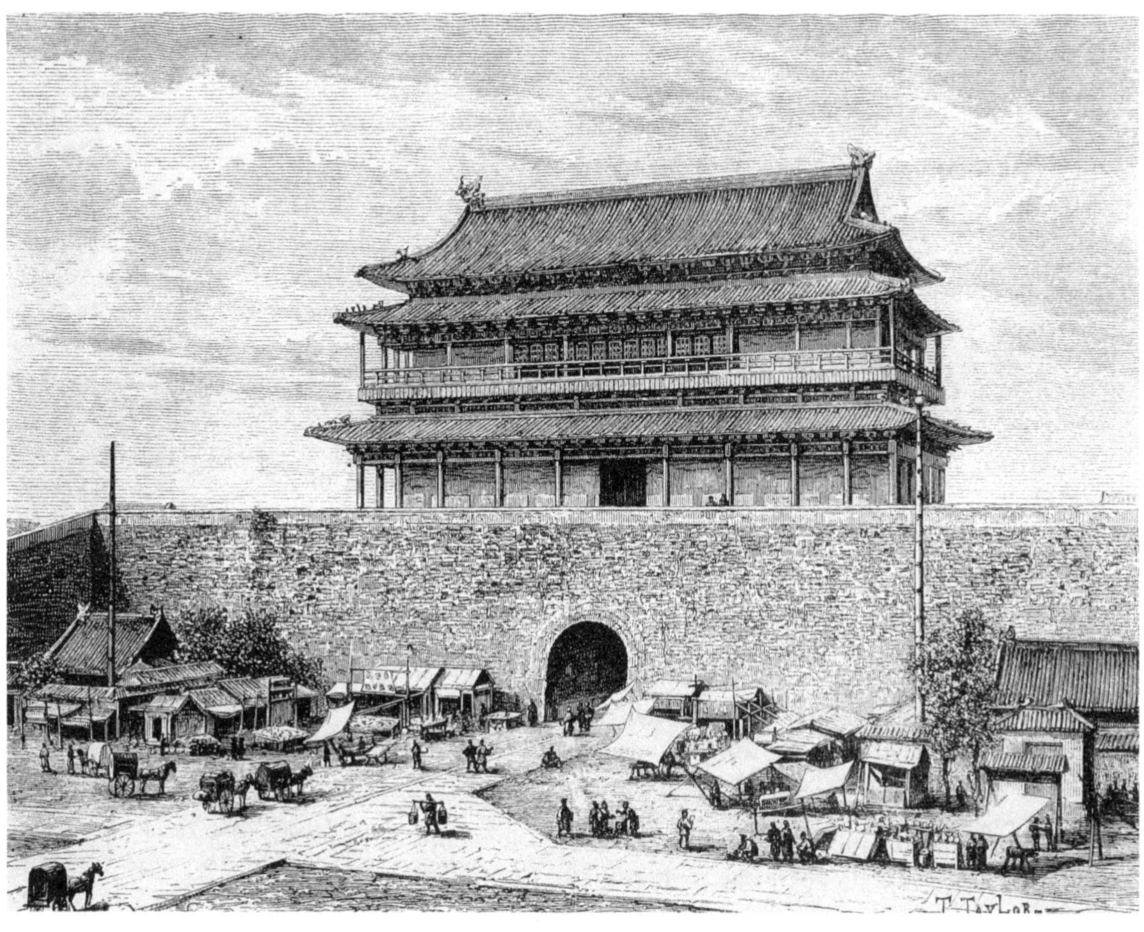

CITY WALL AND GATE SURMOUNTED BY GATE-TOWER.

quietly; but at length, long before we reached the gate, a tall and powerful man, made tenfold more fierce by partial intoxication, let us know that all the militia were not so peaceably inclined, by seizing Mr. Burdon by the shoulders. He endeavoured to shake him off. I turned round to see what was the matter, and in almost no time, we were surrounded by a dozen or a score of these brutal wretches, and were being hurried on to the city at a fearful pace.

"My bag now began to feel very heavy, and I could not change hands to relieve myself. I was soon in a most profuse perspiration, and was scarcely able to keep up with them. We demanded to be taken before the chief magistrate, but were told they knew where to take us to, and what to do with such persons as we were, with the most insulting epithets. The man who first seized Mr. Burdon soon after came to me, and became my principal tormentor; for I was neither so tall nor so strong as my friend, and was therefore less able to resist him. This man all but knocked me down repeatedly, seized me by the hair, took hold of me by the collar so as almost to choke me, grasped my arms and shoulders, making them black and blue; and had this treatment continued much longer, I must have fainted.

All but exhausted, how refreshing was the remembrance of a verse, sent to me by a friend last mail,—

> We speak of the realms of the blest.
> That country so bright and so fair;
> And oft are its glories confest,
> But what must it be to be there!

To be absent from the body! to be present with the LORD! to be free from sin! is surely a wonderful blessing, though not equal to what we shall enjoy after the resurrection. And this is the end of the worst that man's malice can bring upon us.

"While we were walking along, Mr. Burdon tried to give away one or two books that were under his arm, not knowing whether we might have another opportunity of so doing; but the fearful rage of the soldier, who made those who had received them give them up to him, and the way he insisted on manacles being brought (which fortunately were not at hand), convinced us that in our present position we could do no good in attempting book-distribution. There was nothing to be done but to quietly submit, and go along with our captors.

"Once or twice there was a quarrel as to how we should be dealt with; the more mild of our conductors saying we ought to be taken to the magistrate's office, but the others were for killing us at once without appeal to any authority. Our minds were kept in perfect peace; and when thrown together on one of these occasions, we reminded each other that the apostles rejoiced that they were counted *worthy* to suffer in the cause of CHRIST. Having succeeded in getting my hand into my pocket, I got out my Chinese card (if the large red paper, bearing one's name, may be so called), and after its production was treated with more respect. I demanded that this should be given to the chief official of the place, and that we should be led to his office. I also told the man who was tormenting me so, that he had better be cautious how he treated foreigners, and Englishmen; or he might learn some day to his cost, that they were not to be maltreated with impunity. On this he left me and went to Mr. Burdon, to whom he said, with fiendish malice and rage depicted on his countenance, '*You* are no foreigners;' and do what we would, we could not persuade them that we were (though we were both in English attire).

"Oh! the long weary streets that we were dragged through; I thought they never would end; and seldom have I felt more thankful than when we stopped at a place where we were told a mandarin resided.

"Quite exhausted, bathed in perspiration, and with my tongue cleaving to the roof of my mouth, I leaned against the wall; and Mr. Burdon was in much the same state. I requested them to bring us chairs, but they told us to wait; and when I begged them to bring us tea, I received the same answer. Round the door was a very large crowd, and Mr. Burdon, collecting his remaining strength, preached CHRIST JESUS to them. Our cards and the books had been taken in to the mandarin, but he proved to be one of low rank; and, after keeping us waiting some time, he referred us to his superiors in office.

"We were told to go on, but now most positively refused to move a single step, and insisted on sedan chairs being brought. After some demur this was done: we seated ourselves in them, and were carried off. On our way we felt so glad of the rest which the chairs afforded us, and so thankful at having been able to preach JESUS in spite of Satan's malice, that our joy was depicted on our countenances; and, as we passed along, while we heard some say that we did not look like bad men, others seemed to pity us. When we arrived at the magistrate's office, I could not think where we were being carried to: for we passed through some great gates that looked like those of the city wall, but when we got through we were evidently not outside the city. A second pair of gates suggested the idea that it was a prison to which they were taking us: but when we came in sight of a large tablet, on which was inscribed, Ming-chï-fu-mu,—'the father and mother of the people,'—it shewed we were all right, for this is a title assumed by the magistrates.

"Our cards were again sent in, and after a short delay, we were taken into the presence of Chen Ta Lao-ye,—the Great Venerable Father Chen; who, as it proved, had formerly been Tào-tai of Shanghai, and consequently knew the importance of treating foreigners with courtesy.

"On coming before him, some of the people fell on their knees and bowed down to the ground, and my conductor motioned for me to do the same; but, it is needless to say, without

AUDIENCE CHAMBER OF A CHINESE MANDARIN.

success. This mandarin, who seemed to be the highest authority of Tung-chow, and wears an opaque blue button on his cap, came out to meet us, and treated us with every possible token of respect. He took us into an inner apartment, a more private room, but was followed by a large number of writers, runners, and other semi-officials. I related to him the object of our visit, and begged permission to give him a copy of each of our books and tracts, for which he thanked me. As I presented him with copies of the New Testament, part of the Old (from Genesis to Ruth), and some tracts, I gave him a short account of them ; and also gave him a brief summary of our doctrine, telling him that all were sinners, but that JESUS CHRIST, the Son of the only living and true GOD, had come down to this earth and paid our debt on the cross ; that having risen from the dead and ascended into heaven, He is now interceding for us ; that belief in JESUS was the only way to secure everlasting life, and that any works of righteousness that we could do were of no avail to save our souls, &c. He listened very attentively, as, of course did all the others present. He then ordered some refreshments to be brought in, of which he partook with us. These were very welcome to us.

"After a long stay, we asked permission to see something of his city, and to distribute the books we had with us, before our return. To this he consented. We then told him we had been most disrespectfully treated as we came in, but did not think anything of that, as we were aware the soldiers knew no better ; but desiring not to have it repeated, we requested him to give orders that we should not be molested. This also he promised to do ; and, with every possible token of respect, he accompanied us to the door of his official residence, and sent several runners to see that we were respectfully treated. We distributed our books well and quickly, and left the city quite in state.

"It was amusing to see what use the runners made of their tails. When the way was stopped up, they used them as whips, and laid them about the people's shoulders, right and left. We had a little trouble to find our wheel-barrows, but did so eventually ; and paying our chair coolies, mounted the humble vehicles, and returned, accompanied half-way by an attendant from the magistrate's office. Between 6 and 7 p.m., we got back to our boats in safety, sincerely thankful to our HEAVENLY FATHER for His kind aid and protection."

MOORED FOR THE NIGHT.

The next incident to which we will refer, occurred during a missionary journey taken in 1855-6, with the Rev. W. C. Burns, of the English Presbyterian Mission. We reached Wu-chen, or Black Town, in the province of CHEH-KIANG, the inhabitants of which we had been told were the wildest and most lawless people in that part of the country. Such we found them to be: the town was indeed a refuge for salt-smugglers and other bad characters.

"*January 8th*, 1856.—Commenced our work in Wu-chen this morning by distributing about 300 handbill tracts, and some Testaments. The people seemed much surprised, and we could not learn that any foreigner had been here before. We preached twice, once in the temple of Kwan-ti, and afterwards in an empty space left by a fire, which had completely destroyed a great many houses. In the afternoon we preached again to a large and attentive audience, on the same site; and in the evening we all went to a tea-shop, where we had a good opportunity of speaking for some time: but it got noised abroad that we were there, and too many people coming in, we had to leave. The native assistants, Dzien and Kway-hwo, were, however, able to remain. On our way back, we spoke to a number of people on a bridge, for a short time; and had abundant reason to be thankful and encouraged by the result of our first day's labours.

A CHINESE HORIZONTAL BRIDGE.

"*January 10th.*—First sent Dzien and Kway-hwo to distribute some sheet tracts. After their return we went along with them, and, in a space cleared by fire, we separated, and addressed two audiences. On our return to our boats for lunch, we found, as usual, people waiting and desiring books. Some were distributed to those who were able to use them; and then, desiring the people to wait till we took our lunch, I went into my boat and closed the door. I had only just poured out a cup of tea, when a battering began, and the roof was at once broken in. I went out at the back, and saw four or five men taking the large lumps of frozen earth turned up in a field close by, and weighing, I should suppose, from seven to fourteen pounds each, and throwing them at the boat. Speaking to them was of no use; and it was not long ere, by this means, and by battering at the side with the plank placed to walk on and off by, a considerable part of the *house* of the boat was broken to pieces, and no small quantity of earth covered the things inside. Finally, Dzien got a small boat that was passing to land him at a short distance, and by a few tracts he drew our assailants away, and thus ended the assault.

"We now learned that, of those who had done this mischief, only two were natives of the place, the other three being salt-smugglers; and that the cause was our not having satisfied their unreasonable demand for books. Most providentially, no one was injured; and, as soon as quiet was somewhat restored, we all met in Mr. Burns's boat, and joined in thanksgiving that we had been preserved from personal harm, prayed for the perpetrators of the mischief, and that it might be overruled for good to us and to those with us. We then took our lunch, and afterwards went on shore; and but a few steps from our boats, addressed the large multitude who soon assembled. We were specially assisted; never were we heard with more attention; and not one voice was sympathizing with the men who had molested us. In the evening also, in the tea-shop, the same spirit was manifested, and some seemed to hear with joy the glad tidings of salvation through a crucified SAVIOUR. As we came home, we passed a barber's shop still open, and I went in; and while getting my head shaved, had an opportunity of speaking to a few people, and had a couple of sheet tracts pasted on the walls for future customers to see.

"*January 11th.*—A respectable shopkeeper, of the name of Yao, received from us, on the first or second day of our stay at Wu-chen, a portion of the New Testament and a tract; and yesterday, when our boat was broken, he came to beg for some more books. At that time we were all in confusion from the damage done, and from the earth thrown into the boat; we therefore desired him to come again in a day or two, when we would supply him. He came this morning and handed in the following note:—

"'On a former day, I begged Burns and Taylor, the two *Rabbis*, to give me good books. It happened that at that time those of our town whose hearts were deceived by *Satan*, not knowing *the Son of David*, went so far as to dare to *raca* and *moreh* and injure your respected boat. I thank you for promising afterwards to give the books, and beg the following,—Complete New Testament, Discourse of a Good Man when near his Death, Important Christian Doctrines, Almanac, Principles of Christianity, Way to Make the World Happy,—of each one copy. Sung and Dzien, and all teachers, I hope are well. Further compliments are unwritten.'

"The note is interesting, as shewing that he had been reading the New Testament attentively, as the italicized words were all taken from it. His use of *raca* and *moreh* for reviling, shews their meaning was not lost upon him.

"After supplying this man, we went out with Dzien and Kway-hwo into the east of the town, and in the street spoke for a short time. After our return to the boats, I was called upon by two CHIH-LI men, who are in the magistrate's office here. I was greatly assisted in speaking to them of a crucified Saviour, &c., in the mandarin dialect; and though one of them did not pay much attention, the other did, and made enquiries that shewed the interest he was taking. After they left, I went on shore; and spoke to the people collected there, as soon as Kway-hwo, who was then speaking, concluded. The topic on which I had just been dwelling had moved my own heart, and I was aided in speaking, while the audience was most quiet and attentive. The sun, just setting, afforded a parable, and reminded me of the words of JESUS, 'The night cometh when no man can work;' and as I spoke of the uncertain duration of life, and of our ignorance as to the time of CHRIST's return, a degree of deep seriousness prevailed that I had never previously seen in China. I engaged in prayer, and the greatest decorum was observed. I then went into my boat, with a Buddhist priest who had been hearing me; and he admitted that Buddhism was a system of deceit and could give no hope in death.

"*January 12th.*—In the afternoon we addressed the people on shore, opposite our boats; also in one of the streets, and in a tea-shop, books being distributed on each occasion. In the evening we went out as usual to speak in the tea-shops; but determined to go to the opposite end of the town (it was a straggling place, nearly two English miles long), in order to afford those who lived there a better opportunity of meeting with us. As Mr. Burns and I were accustomed to talk together in Chinese, this conclusion was known to those in the boats.

"After we had proceeded a short distance on our way, we changed our minds and went, instead, to the usual tea-shop, thinking that persons might have gone there on purpose to meet us. But this was not the case; and we did not find such serious hearers as we had done on previous occasions. On this account, Mr. Burns proposed leaving earlier than usual, and we did so; telling Dzien and Kway-hwo that they might remain a little longer. On our way back to the boats we gave away a few books; but, singularly enough, we were left to return alone,—no one going with us, as is generally the case. Instead of being a clear night, as it was when we left the boats, we found that it had become intensely dark. On our way we met the boatman, whose manner seemed very strange; and, without giving us any explanation, he blew out our lantern candle. We relighted the lantern, telling him he was not to put it out again; when, to our surprise, he took the candle out and threw it into the canal. He then walked down on a low wall jutting to the water's edge, and looked into the water.

"Not knowing what was the matter with him, I ran forward to hold him, fearful lest he was going to drown himself; but to my great relief he came back. In answer to our repeated enquiries, he told us not to speak, for some bad men were seeking to destroy the boats, and they had moved them off to avoid this. He then led us to the place where one of them was lying. Before long, Dzien and Kway-hwo came, and got safely on board; and soon after we were joined by the teacher Sung, and the boat moved off.

"The cause of all this disturbance was then explained:—A man, professing to be the constable, had come to the boats in our absence, with a written demand for ten dollars and a quantity of opium. He stated that there were more than fifty country people (salt smugglers) awaiting our reply in an adjoining tea-shop; that if we gave them what they wanted, and three hundred cash to pay for their tea, we might remain in peace; but if not, they would come at once and destroy our boats. Sung told them that we could not comply with their demand; for not doing any trade, but only preaching and distributing books, we had not an atom of opium; and that our money was nearly expended; a fact of which he was aware (as far as I was concerned), as I had been saying to them that I should have to return to Shanghai for supplies early next week. The man, however, told him plainly that he did not believe him; and Sung had no alternative but to seek us, desiring the man to await our reply. Not knowing that we had changed our plan, he sought us in the wrong direction, and, of course, in vain.

"In the meantime the boatmen succeeded in moving off. They were very much alarmed; and had had such a proof but a few days before of what these men dare do in open day-light, that they had no desire to see what they would do by night. They had moved off, therefore, and separated, one going to one place, and the other to another; that if one boat should be injured, the other might afford us a refuge. It was after this that we so providentially met the boatman, and were led on board. As Sung repassed the place where the boats had been lying, he saw between ten and twenty men among the trees, and heard them enquiring where the boats had gone to, but no one knew. Fortunately, they sought in vain.

"Moving to the west, the two boats joined, and rowed together for some time. It was already late; and to travel by night in that part of the country was not the way to avoid danger from evil men; so the question came, what was to be done? This we left for the boatmen to decide: they had moved off of themselves, and we felt that whatever we might personally do, we could not constrain others to remain in a dangerous position. We told them, however, what they did, to do quickly, as the morrow was the Lord's-day, and we did not wish to travel on it: we also informed them, that wherever we were, we must fulfil our mission, and preach the gospel; it therefore was a very little matter where we stayed, because, if we passed the night unperceived, we were sure to be found out on the following day. The men consequently said, 'We might as well return to the place where we started,'—to which we replied, 'Decidedly so;' and they turned back accordingly. But, whether intentionally or accidentally I know not, they got into another stream, and rowed they knew not whither for some time, it being very dark; and at last they moored for the night. We then called all the boatmen together, with our native assistants, and read to them the ninety-first Psalm. It may be imagined how appropriate to our position and need, and how sweetly consoling was this portion of GOD's word:—

'He that dwelleth in the secret place of the MOST HIGH.
'Shall abide under the shadow of the ALMIGHTY.
'I will say of the LORD, *He* is my refuge and my fortress:
'My GOD; in Him will I trust.

'Surely He shall deliver thee from the snare of the fowler,
'And from the noisome pestilence.
'He shall cover thee with His feathers, and under His wings shalt thou trust:
'His truth shall be thy shield and buckler.
'Thou shalt not be afraid for the terror by night;
'Nor for the arrow that flieth by day.'

* * * * *

'Because he hath set his love upon Me, therefore will I deliver him.
'I will set him on high, because he hath known My name.
'He shall call upon Me, and I will answer him;
'I will be with him in trouble;—I will deliver him, and honour him.
'With long life will I satisfy him,—and shew him My salvation.'

"Committing ourselves in prayer to His care and keeping who had covered us with thick darkness and permitted us to escape from the hand of the violent, we retired for the night; which—thanks to the kind protection of the WATCHMAN OF ISRAEL, who neither slumbers nor forgets His people—we passed in peace and quietness, and were enabled, in some measure, to realise the truth of that precious word, '*Thou* art my *Hiding place*, and my *Shield*.'

"*Sunday, January* 13*th*.—I was awakened this morning at about 4 a.m., by a violent pain in the knee joint. I had bruised it the day before, and severe inflammation had resulted. To my great surprise, I heard the rain pouring down in torrents, the weather having previously been particularly fine. We found ourselves so near our former stopping place, that had nothing happened to prevent, we should not have felt justified in neglecting to go into the town to preach as usual. But the rain was so heavy all day that no one could leave the boats. We enjoyed, therefore, a delightful day of rest, such as I have not had for some time; and the weather, doubtless, prevented much enquiry for us; whereas, had the day been fine, we should most likely have been discovered, even if we had not left our boats. As it was, we were allowed to think in peace, with wonder and gratitude, of the gracious dealings of our GOD, who had thus led us 'apart into a desert place,' to 'rest awhile.'

"*January* 14*th*.—A cloudless morning. One of the native assistants went this morning before day-break to get some clothes which had been put out to wash. He came back with the tidings, that notwithstanding the drenching rain of yesterday, men had been seeking us in all directions. We, however, had been kept in safety 'under the shadow of the ALMIGHTY.' The boatmen were now so frightened that they would remain no longer, and moved off at dawn. I was confined to my boat by lameness, and had no alternative but to go with them. In the afternoon we reached Ping-wang."

The incidents narrated above, exemplify GOD's preserving care in circumstances of external peril. There are other difficulties to which persons labouring in the interior of China may be exposed, which do not come under this class. Their funds may become exhausted when far in the interior; and communication with the free ports may be difficult or impossible. Or they may be robbed of all that they possess, and may find themselves destitute in the midst of strangers. But they cannot be robbed of His presence and aid, whose are the gold and the silver, and the cattle on a thousand hills. And His promise, that if we seek first the kingdom of GOD and His righteousness all needful temporal blessings shall be added, will be as reliable under these circumstances as when every external blessing abounds. GOD's arm is never shortened that it cannot save; and it is still true, that man doth not live by bread alone,—although this may be the ordinary means which GOD employs to sustain life. The hearts of all men are under His control: *He* can soften the hardest heart, and give help to His servants, by means through which it was least expected. We give one more extract from our journal for 1856. The occasion was an attempted missionary journey from Shanghai to Ningpo, *via* Hang-chau, in which the writer was alone. After fourteen days spent in travelling, preaching, and distributing books, we reached a large town called Shih-mun-wan.

"*August 4th.*—My books were all distributed. During the journey I had given away upwards of 200 Testaments, 1200 tracts, and 1600 handbills. I now, therefore, determined to make all haste to Ningpo, *via* Hai-ning Chau.

"There was no water beyond Shih-mun-wan, so I paid off my boat, hired coolies to carry my things to Chang-gan, and ere sun-rise set off. I walked on first, leaving my servant to follow with the coolies, who made frequent stoppages to rest, and when I reached Shih-mun Hian, I waited for them in the first tea-shop outside the North Gate. The coolies came on very slowly; but after a while they arrived, and said they were very tired. I found they were opium-smokers: and though there were two of them, and they had only carried a load for eighteen *li* (about six miles) which one strong man is in the habit of carrying fifty *li*, they really seemed weary. When they had taken some rice and tea, and had had an hour's rest (and I doubt not, a smoke of the opium pipe) they seemed refreshed; and I proposed moving on that we might get to Chang-gan ere the sun was too powerful. My servant had a friend in Shih-mun Hian, and he desired to spend the day there, and go on next morning; but to this I objected, as I wished to reach Hai-ning Chau that night, where we could get sedan chairs for ourselves; and new coolies would be procurable at Chang-gan for the latter part of the journey. We therefore set off, entered the city together, and passed about a third of the way through it, when the coolies stopped to rest, and said they should be unable to carry the burden through to Chang-gan; so it was agreed that they should take it to the South Gate, and be paid in proportion to the distance they had carried it, and that the servant should call other coolies and come along with them.

"I walked on before as in the first instance, and the distance only being twelve *li*, got to Chang-gan, and waited their arrival, meanwhile engaging coolies for the journey to Hai-ning Chau. Having waited a long time, I began to wonder at their delay; and at last it became too late to finish the journey to Hai-ning that day. I felt somewhat annoyed; and had not

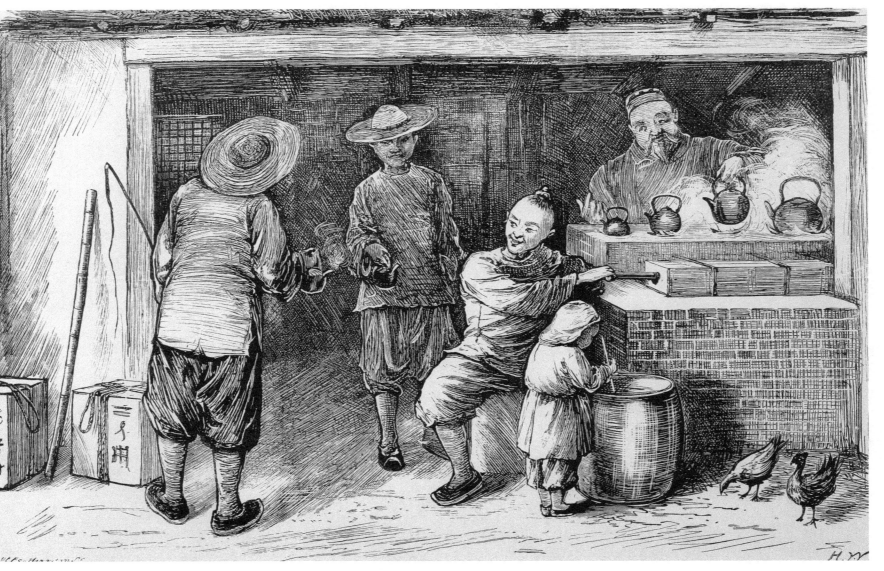

A CHINESE INN.

my feet been blistered and the day very hot, should have gone back to meet them and urge them on. I then thought that my servant must have gone to his friend's, and would not come till evening. But evening came, and no appearance of them.

"I began to feel very uneasy, and enquired everywhere if they had been seen. At last a person said, 'Are you a guest from Shih-mun-wan?' I answered in the affirmative. 'Are you going to Hai-ning?' 'Yes.' 'Then your things have gone on before you; for I was sitting in a tea-shop when a coolie came in, took a cup of tea, and set off for Hai-ning in a great hurry, saying the bamboo box and bed he carried, which were like what you describe yours to be, were from Shih-mun-wan, and he had to carry them to Hai-ning to-night, when he was to be paid at the rate of ten cash a pound.' From this I concluded my goods were before me: but it was impossible to follow them at once, for I was too tired to walk, and moreover it was already dark.

"Under these circumstances, all I could do was to seek a lodging for the night. This I found no easy matter. I raised my heart to GOD, and asked Him to help me. Then, walking to the further end of the town, where I thought the tidings of there being a foreigner in the place might not have spread, I looked out for a lodging-house. I soon found one, and went in, hoping that I might pass unquestioned,* as it was already dark. Asking the bill of fare, I was told that cold rice (which proved to be more than 'rather burnt'), and snakes fried in lamp-oil, were all that could be had. Not wishing any question to be raised as to my nationality, I was compelled to order some, and tried to make a meal, but with little success. While so engaged, I said to the landlord, 'I suppose I can spend the night here:' to which he replied in the affirmative.

"Bringing out his book, he said, 'In these unsettled times we are required by the authorities to keep a record of our lodgers: may I ask your respected family name?' I replied, 'My unworthy family name is Tai.' 'And your honourable name?' 'My humble name is Yuô-kôh (James). 'What an extraordinary name! I never heard it before. How do you write it?' I told him; and added, 'It is a common name where I come from.' 'And may I ask whence you come, and whither you are going?' 'I am journeying from Shanghai to Ningpo, by way of Hang-chau. 'What may be your honourable profession? 'I heal the sick.' 'Oh! you are a physician,' the landlord remarked, and to my intense relief closed the book.

"His wife, however, took up the conversation. 'You are a physician, are you?' said she; 'I am glad of that, for I have a daughter afflicted with leprosy. If you will cure her, you shall have your supper and bed for nothing.' I was curious enough to enquire here what my supper and bed were to cost, if paid for; and to my amusement found they were to be about 1¼d. of our money! Being unable to benefit the girl, I declined to prescribe for her, saying that leprosy was a very intractable disease, and that I had no medicines with me. The mother brought pen and paper, saying, 'You can at least write a prescription, which will do no harm, if it does no good.' This also I declined to do, and requested to be shewn my bed.

"I was conducted to a very miserable room on the ground floor, where, on some boards raised on two stools, I passed the night, without bed or pillow, save my umbrella and shoe, and without any mosquito curtains. There were sleeping in the same room ten or eleven other lodgers, so I could not take anything off, for fear of its being stolen: but I found I was by no means too warm as midnight came on.

"*August 5th.*—As may be supposed, I arose but little rested or refreshed, and felt very unwell. I had to wait a long time ere I could get my breakfast, and then there was another delay before I could get the only dollar I had in my pocket changed, from its having one or two chops on it. More than 300 cash were deducted from its price, which was a serious loss in my present position. I then sought through the town for tidings of my servant and coolies, as I thought it most likely, if the report I had heard last night of their passing was not correct, that they would have arrived

* The writer was now wearing the Chinese costume.

later last night, or come in the morning. The town is large, long, and straggling, being nearly two miles from one end to the other, so this took me some time.

"I gained no information, so I set off for Hai-ning Chau, wearied and footsore, in the full heat of the sun. The journey (25 *li*) took me a long time; but a village half-way, Shih-sing, afforded a resting-place and a cup of tea, of both of which I gladly availed myself. When about to leave it, a shower of rain came on, heavy but short. The delay occasioned by this, enabled me to address a few words to the people.

"The afternoon was far spent before I approached the northern suburb of Hai-ning Chau, where I commenced enquiring, but heard no tidings of my servant or things. I was told that outside the East Gate I should be more likely to hear of them, as it was there the sea-junks called; I therefore proceeded thither, and sought for them outside the Little East Gate, but in vain. Very weary, I sat down in a tea-shop to rest; and while there, a number of persons from one of the Ya-muns (mandarins' offices) came in, and made enquiries as to who I was, where I had come from, &c., &c. On learning the object of my search, one of the men in the tea-shop said, 'A bamboo box and a bed, such as you describe, were carried past here about half-an-hour ago; the bearer seemed to be going towards either the Great East, or the South Gate: you had better go to the hongs there and enquire.' I asked him to accompany me in the search, and promised to reward him for his trouble; but he would not. Another man offered to go with me, so we set off together, and both inside and outside the two gates made diligent enquiries, but in vain. I then engaged a man to make a thorough search, promising him a liberal reward if he should be successful. In the meantime I had some dinner, and addressed a large concourse of people who had gathered together.

"When he returned from a fruitless search, I said to him, 'I am quite exhausted—will you help me to find quarters for the night, and then I will pay you for your trouble?' He said, 'Yes' and we set off in search of lodgings. At the first place or two at which we enquired, they would not receive me—for though on our first enquiring they seemed willing to do so, the presence of a man who followed us, and who, I found, was engaged in one of the Ya-muns, seemed to alarm them, and I was refused. We now went to a third place, and being no longer followed by the Ya-mun people, we were promised quarters: some tea was brought, and I paid the man who had accompanied me for his trouble. Soon after he was gone, some of the people of the Ya-mun came in; they soon went away, but the result of their visit was, that I was told I could not be entertained there. A young man blamed them for their heartless behaviour, and said to me, 'Never mind, come with me, and if we cannot get better lodgings for you, you shall sleep at our house.'

"I went with him, but we found the people of his house unwilling to receive me. Weary and footsore, so that I could scarcely put one foot before the other, I had again to seek quarters, and at length got promise of them; but some people collecting about the door, they desired me to go to a tea-shop and wait there till the people had retired, or they would be unable to accommodate me. There was no help for it, so we went and waited till past midnight; then we left for the promised resting-place, but my conductor *would* not find it; he led me about to another part of the city, and finally, between 1 and 2 a.m., left me to pass the night as well as I could.

"I was opposite a temple, but it was closed; so I lay down on the stone steps in front of it, and putting my money under my head for a pillow, should soon have been asleep in spite of the cold, had I not perceived a person coming stealthily towards me. As he approached, I saw he was one of the beggars so common in China, and I had no doubt his intention was to rob me of my money. I did not stir, but watched his movements, and looked to my FATHER not to leave me in this time of trial. The man came up, looked at me for some time to assure himself I was asleep (it was so dark he could not see that my eyes were fixed on him), and then began to feel about me gently. I said to him in the quietest tone, but so as to

THE STEPS IN FRONT OF A CHINESE TEMPLE.

convince him I was not, nor had been, sleeping, 'What do you want?' He made no answer, but went away.

"I was very thankful to see him go, and when he was out of sight, put as much of my cash as would not go into my pocket into my sleeve, and made my pillow of a stone projection of the wall. It was not long ere I began to doze, but was aroused by the all but noiseless footsteps of two persons approaching—for my

nervous system was rendered so sensitive by exhaustion, that the slightest noise startled me. I again sought protection from Him who alone was my stay, and lay still as before; till one of them came up and began to feel under my head for the cash. I spoke again—they sat down at my feet. I asked them what they were doing; they replied that they, like me, were going to pass the night there. I then requested them to take the opposite side, as there was plenty of room, and leave this side to me; but they would not move from my feet, so I raised myself up, and set my back against the wall. They said, 'You had better lie down and sleep; if you do not you will be unable to walk to-morrow. Do not be afraid; we shall not leave you, and will see no one hurts you.' I replied, 'Listen to me: I do not want your protection—I need it not, I am not a Chinese—I do not worship your senseless, helpless idols. I worship GOD—He is my FATHER—I trust in Him. I know well what *you* are, and what your intentions are, and shall keep my eye on you and shall not sleep.'

"On this, one of them went away, but soon returned with a third companion. I felt very uneasy, but looked to GOD for help: once or twice one of them got up to see if I was asleep. I said, 'Do not be mistaken, I am not sleeping.' Occasionally my head dropped, and this was a signal for one of them to rise; but I at once roused myself and made some remark. As the night slowly passed on, I felt very sleepy; and to keep myself awake, as well as to cheer my mind, I sang several hymns, repeated aloud some portions of Scripture, and engaged in prayer in English—to the great annoyance of my companions, who seemed as if they would have given anything to get me to desist. After that they troubled me no more; and shortly before dawn of day they left me, and I got a little sleep.

"*August 6th.*—I was awakened by the young man who had led me about so the previous evening. He was very rude, and insisted on my getting up and paying him for his trouble last night; and even went so far as to try to accomplish by force what he wanted. It quite roused me; and in an unguarded moment, with very improper feeling, I seized his arm with such a grasp as he little expected I was capable of, and dared him to lay a finger on me again or to annoy me. This quite changed his manner; he let me quietly remain till the guns announced the opening of the gates of the city; then he begged me, at least, to give him some money to buy opium with. It is needless to say he was refused. I gave him the price of two candles he said he had burnt while with me last night, and no more. I learned he was connected with one of the Ya-muns.

"As soon as I could, I bought some rice-gruel and tea for breakfast, and then once more made a personal search after my things. Some hours thus spent proving unavailing, I set out on my return; and after a long, weary, and painful walk, reached Chang-gan about noon. My enquiries here also failed to give me any trace of my missing goods and man; so I had a meal cooked in a tea-shop, got a thorough wash and bathed my inflamed feet, and after my dinner rested and slept till 4 p.m. Much refreshed by this, I set off for Shih-mun Hien. On the way I was led to reflect on the goodness of GOD, and recollected that I had not made it a matter of prayer that I should be provided with lodgings last night. I felt condemned, too, that I should have been so anxious for my few things, while the many precious souls around me had caused so little emotion. I came as a sinner, pleaded the blood of JESUS, felt I was accepted in Him—pardoned, cleansed, sanctified. And oh! the love of JESUS—how great I felt it to be! I knew something more than I had known before of what it was to be despised and rejected; not to have where to lay my head; and felt more than ever I had done before, the greatness of that love which induced *Him* to leave His throne, and to suffer thus for me—nay, to lay down His life on the cross. I thought of *Him* as despised and rejected of men, a Man of sorrows and acquainted with grief—at times without a place to lay *His* head. I thought of Him at Jacob's well, weary, hungry, and thirsty, yet finding it His meat and drink to do His FATHER'S will; and contrasted this with my littleness of love. I looked to Him for pardon for the past and for grace and strength to do His will in the future, to tread more closely in His footsteps, and be more than ever wholly His. I prayed for myself, for friends in England, and for my brethren in the work. Sweet tears of mingled joy and sorrow flowed freely, the road was almost forgotten, and ere I was aware of it, I was close to Shih-mun Hien. Outside the South Gate I took a cup of tea, asked about my lost luggage, and spoke of the love of JESUS. Then I entered the city, and after many vain enquiries left it by the North Gate.

"I felt so much refreshed both in mind and body by the communion I had had on my walk to the city, that I thought myself able to walk over to Shih-mun-wan that evening. I first went into another tea-shop and bought some cakes, &c., and was making a meal of them, when who should come in but one of the coolies who had carried my things the first stage. From him I learned that after I left them they carried my luggage to the South Gate; then my servant went out, and said on his return that I was gone on, and he did not intend to go at once, but would spend the day with his friend, and then rejoin me. They carried the things to this friend's house and left them there. I got him to go with me to the house, and there learned he had spent the day and night with them, and next morning had called coolies and set off for Hang-chau. This was all I could learn; so, unable to do anything but proceed on my way to Shanghai with all expedition, I left the city again: but it was now too late to go on. I looked to my FATHER, as able to supply *all* my need, and received another token of His ceaseless care and love, being invited to sleep on a hong-boat now dry in the bed of the river. The night was again very cold, and the mosquitoes troublesome; still I got a little rest, and at sun-rise was up and continued my journey.

"*August 7th*—I felt very ill at first, and had a sore throat, but reflected on the wonderful goodness of GOD in enabling me to bear the heat by day and the cold by night so long; and as I soon began to freely perspire from walking, became relieved. I felt now, too, that quite a load was taken off my mind. *I had committed myself and my affairs to the* LORD, and knew that if it was for my good and His glory, my things would be restored; if not, all would be for the best. I hoped that the most trying part of my journey was now drawing to a close, and this helped me, weary and footsore, on the way. When I got to Shih-mun-wan and had breakfasted, I found I had still 810 cash* in hand; and I knew the hong-boat fare to Kia-hing Fu was 120 cash, and thence to Shanghai 360, leaving me 330 cash for three or four days' provisions. I went at once to the boat-office; but to my dismay found that from the dry state of the river goods had not come down, so that no boat would leave to-day, perhaps not to-morrow. I enquired if there were no letter-boats for Kia-hing Fu, and was told they had already left. My only resource, therefore, was to ascertain if any private boats were going in which I could get a passage. My search was in vain; and I could get no boat to go all the way to Shanghai, or my difficulty would have been at an end. But at a place where the canal takes a turn, I saw before me a letter-boat going in the direction of Kia-hing Fu. This, I thought, must be one of the Kia-hing Fu boats, that had been detained by something; and I set off after it as fast as hope and the necessities of my case could take me. For the time, fatigue and sore feet were forgotten. After a chase of a mile I overtook it. 'Are you going to Kia-hing Fu?' I called out. 'No.' 'Are you going in that direction?' 'No.' 'Will you give me a passage as far as you do go that way?' 'No.' Completely dispirited and exhausted, I sunk down on the grass, and fainted away.

"As consciousness returned, some voices reached my ear, and I found they were talking about me. One said, 'He speaks unmixed Shanghai dialect,' and from their own speech I knew they were Shanghai people. Raising my umbrella, I saw they were on a large hong-boat on the other side of the canal, and after a few words they sent their small boat for me, and I went on board the junk. They were very kind, gave me some tea, and, when I was

* About 20 cash make a penny.

somewhat refreshed and able to partake of it, some food. I then took my shoes and stockings off and eased my feet, the boatmen kindly providing me with hot water to bathe them. When they heard my story, and saw the blisters on my feet, they evidently pitied me, and hailed every boat that passed to see if it was going my way. Not getting one, by and bye, after a few hours' sleep, I went ashore with the captain, intending to preach in the temple of Kwanti.

"Before leaving the boat, I had told the captain and those on board that I was now unable to help myself. That I had not strength to walk to Kia-hing Fu, and having been disappointed in getting a passage to-day, I should no longer have sufficient means to take me there by letter-boat (an expensive mode of travelling). That I knew not *how* the God whom I served would help me, but that I had no doubt He would do so; and that my business now was to serve Him where I was. I also told them that the relief which I knew would come, ought to be an evidence to them of the truth of the religion which I and the other missionaries at Shanghai preached.

"On our way to the town, while the captain and I were engaged in conversation together, we saw a letter-boat coming up. The captain drew my attention to it; but I reminded him that I had no longer the means of paying my passage by it. He hailed it, nevertheless, and found that it was going to a place about nine English miles from Shanghai, whence one of the boatmen would carry the mails over-land to Shanghai. He then said, 'This gentleman is a foreigner from Shanghai, who has been robbed and has no longer the means of returning. If you will take him with you as far as you go, and then engage a sedan chair to take him the rest of the way, he will pay you in Shanghai. You see my boat is lying aground yonder for want of water, and cannot get away. Now, I will stand surety, and if this gentleman does not pay you when you get to Shanghai, I will do so on your return.' This unsolicited kindness on the part of a Chinaman, a perfect stranger, will appear the more remarkable to anyone acquainted with the character of the Chinese, who are generally most reluctant to part with their money.

"Those on the letter-boat agreeing to the terms, I was taken on board as a passenger. Oh! how thankful I felt for this providential interposition, and to be once more on my way to Shanghai. These letter-boats are very small inside, being long and narrow; one has to lie down all the time they are going, as a very little thing would upset them. This was no objection to me; on the contrary, I was but too glad to lie down. They are the quickest Chinese boats I have seen. Each one has two men, who work in turns, night and day: they row with their feet and paddle with their hands; or if the wind is quite fair, row with their feet, with one hand manage a small sail, and steer with the other. After a pleasant and speedy journey, I reached Shanghai in safety, on the 9th of August, through the help of Him who has said, 'I will never leave thee, nor forsake thee;' 'Lo, I am with you alway, even unto the end of the world.'"

Many other incidents might be given, all tending to prove that in the absence of ordinary means, God can and does help His servants in their difficulties. Let but devoted labourers be found, who will prove faithful to God, and there is no reason to fear that God will not prove faithful to them. He will set before them an open door; and will esteem them of more value than the sparrows and the lilies which He feeds and clothes. He will be with them in danger, in difficulty, in perplexity; and while *they* may be perfect weakness, *He* will work in them mightily. They may cast their bread upon the waters, but His word shall not return unto Him void, but shall accomplish that which He pleases, and shall prosper in the thing whereto He sends it.

Nineteen years ago we gave the above instances of GOD's direct interposition in times of peril and need, to warrant our expectation that GOD would provide both the men and the means for carrying His blessed gospel into each of the unevangelized provinces of China Proper and into Chinese Tartary. Upon past EBENEZERS we built our JEHOVAH-JIREH. "They that know Thy name will put their trust in Thee." The experience of these nineteen years abundantly shews how safe it has been to base our expectations on the promises of the living GOD.

And first, as to the labourers themselves. As in the beginning of the gospel there was need of, and work for, a Paul, an Apollos, a Luke, as well as those who were manifestly "unlearned and ignorant," but of whom men "took knowledge that they had been with JESUS,"—so it is now. The LORD can sanctify and use every talent that He has bestowed; He also can, and often does choose "the foolish things of the world to confound the wise, and the weak things of the world to confound the things which are mighty." Some who have gone out have had special philological talent, others have had deeper acquaintance with GOD's Word and more matured Christian experience; but each one, we believe, has been qualified for that sphere of service which the LORD intended him or her to occupy. So we expect it will be. We have already shewn that many of the spoken languages of China are easy of acquisition, and that the mass of the people can neither read nor write; this being the case it is obvious that persons of moderate ability and limited attainments are not precluded from engaging in the work: and we shall most gladly enter into correspondence with any such who may feel called to it. At the same time, there is ample scope for the exercise of the highest talent that can be laid upon the altar of GOD. Nay more, there is an urgent call for men filled with love to GOD, whose superior education will enable them to occupy spheres of usefulness into which others could not enter. The proposed field is so extensive, and the need of labourers of every class is so great, that "the eye cannot say to the hand, 'I have no need of thee,' nor again the head to the feet, 'I have no need of you.'"

As to those who feel themselves called to the work, the plan we were led to adopt, and on which the blessing of GOD has evidently rested, was and now is as follows:—After correspondence with and about them, personal acquaintance has been sought, and every care has been taken to ascertain whether they have been called to, and fitted for, the work. In order to know them more thoroughly, they have been invited to reside for a longer or shorter time with us. When the writer, and other Christian friends, have been satisfied of the fitness of one and another for the work in China, the LORD has been asked to open the way, and provide the means for outfit and passage; and He has answered prayer. By GOD'S help, we purpose to continue working on the same plan, and to help out none who are not personally known to us, or to those who superintend the home department of our work.

Our work is evangelistic and unsectarian: we desire to win souls for CHRIST, and not to spread any particular views of church government. The LORD has given us as helpers, persons from most if not all of the leading denominations of England and Scotland.

For the convenience of carrying on the work, an account was opened with the London and County Bank. For this purpose it was necessary to adopt a definite name, and that of the "CHINA INLAND MISSION" was adopted as being the most suitable, seeing our great desire and aim were to plant the standard of the cross in the eleven provinces of China Proper previously unoccupied, and in Chinese Tartary. How far this hope has been realised may be learned in some measure from what follows. It may however be well to point out here, that as it was absolutely necessary to have a basis from which to ramify, and as we had such a basis in the CHEH-KIANG province, we did not, in adopting the title "China Inland Mission," propose to abandon the work there. On the contrary, we hoped to see it carried on with greater blessing than ever, and in this too our expectation has not been disappointed, for none that wait on GOD shall be ashamed.

TEMPLE OF HEAVEN, PEKIN.

APPENDIX A.

LIST OF PROTESTANT MISSIONARIES IN CHINA IN 1884.

This list is based mainly on one published in "*The Shanghai Missionary Recorder.*" The Societies are arranged as in our Conspectus on pages 40, 41, in the order in which the Society or Denomination commenced work in China. The names of the Male Missionaries are given in Small Capitals (CHINA); those of Medical Missionaries are in blacker type (**China**); and Ordained Medical Missionaries in blacker Capitals (**CHINA**). Lady Missionaries are indicated by Italic Type (*China*); and Medical Ladies by Italic Capitals (*CHINA*). Unmarried men are indicated by an asterisk (*).

ENGLISH SOCIETIES.

LONDON MISSIONARY SOCIETY, 1808.

Pe-kin. — ARRIVAL.

- OWEN, G. S. 1866
- GILMOUR, J. 1870
- MEECH, S. E. 1871
- REES, — 1883
- **Dudgeon, J., M.D.** 1863

Tien-tsin.

- LEES, J. 1861
- KING, A.* 1880
- **Mackenzie, J. K., L.R.C.P., &c.** 1875

Han-kow.

- JOHN, GRIFFITH 1855
- OWEN, W.* 1879
- BONSEY, A.* 1882
- **Gillison, Dr. T.*** 1882

Shang-hai.

- MUIRHEAD, W.* 1847
- STONEHOUSE, J.* 1882

Amoy.

- MACGOWAN, J. 1860
- SADLER, J. 1866
- BUDD, C.* 1876
- BOND, — 1883
- **Palmer, W. S., M.D.*** 1862

Hong-kong.

- CHALMERS, J., LL.D. 1852
- *Rowe, Miss* 1876
- *Hope, Miss* 1882

Canton.

- PEARCE, T. W. 1879
- EICHLER, E. R.* 1881

Absent.

- BRYSON, T. 1866
- EDGE, C. 1874
- **MAWBEY, W., M.D.** 1879

Bible Societies, 1843.

BRITISH AND FOREIGN.

Shang-hai.

- DYER, S., M.A. 1878
- OLSSEN, A. 1882
- MURRAY, D.* 1883
- HARMON, F.* 1883
- UPCROFT, W.* 1883
- WALLEY, J.* 1883

Che-foo.

- BROWN, F.* 1883

Amoy.

- PATON, T. 1882

Hong-kong.

- REINHARDT, J.* 1883

Absent.

- MOLLMAN, J.* 1865

SCOTTISH NATIONAL.

Pe-kin.

- MURRAY, W. H. 1871

Han-kow.

- ARCHIBALD, J. 1877

Chung-k'ing.

- WILSON, JOHN* 1878

Absent.

- BURNETT, R. 1878

Church Missions, 1844.

CHURCH MISSIONARY SOCIETY.

Shang-hai.

- MOULE, A. E. 1861
- LANNING, G. 1875

Ning-po.

- BATES, J. 1867
- HOARE, J. C.* 1874
- *Russell, Mrs.* 1848
- *Laurence, Miss* 1870

Hang-chau.

- MOULE, G. E., D.D. 1858 Bishop of Mid-China
- ELWIN, A. 1870
- **Main, D., M.D.** 1882

Shao-hing.

- VALENTINE, J. D. 1864
- FULLER, A. R. 1882
- HORSBURGH, J. 1883

Foo-chow.

- WOLFE, J. R. 1862
- STEWART, R. W. 1876
- LLOYD, L. 1876
- BANISTER, W. 1881
- SHAW, C.* 1882
- MARTIN, J. R. 1882
- **Taylor, Van S., M.D.** 1878
- *Goldie, Miss* 1882

Hong-kong.

- BURDON, J. S., D.D. 1853 Bishop of South China
- OST, J. B. 1880

Canton.

- GRUNDY, J. 1878

Absent.

- SEDGWICK, J. H.* 1874
- SHANN, R. 1879
- NASH, C. B.* 1881

SOCIETY FOR PROPAGATION OF THE GOSPEL.

Pe-kin.

- BRERETON, W. 1875

Che-foo.

- SCOTT, C. P., D.D.* 1874 Bishop of North China
- GREENWOOD, M.* 1874
- CORFE, C. J.* 1881
- HILDESLEY, W.* 1881
- VINCENT, J. R.* 1881

Presbyterian Missions, 1848.

ENGLISH.

Amoy.

- SWANSON, W. S. 1860
- MCGREGOR, W. 1864
- THOMPSON, H. 1877
- WATSON, J. 1880
- **Grant, D., M.B., C.M.** 1880
- **MACLEISH, A.L., M.B.** 1881
- *Maclagan, Miss* 1883

T'ai-wan.

- CAMPBELL, W. 1871
- THOW, W.* 1881
- THOMPSON, W. R. 1883
- **Anderson, P., L.R.C.P., &c.** 1880
- *Ritchie, Mrs.* 1867
- *Murray, Miss* 1880

Swa-tow.

- SMITH, G.* 1857
- MACKENZIE, H. L. 1860
- DUFFUS, W. 1869
- MCIVER, D.* 1879
- PATON, W. 1881
- **Lyall, A., M.B., C.M.** 1879
- **RIDDELL, W., M.B., C.M.** 1881
- *Ricketts, Miss* 1878

Absent.

- GORDON, R. 1872
- BARCLAY, T. 1874
- GIBSON, J. C. 1874
- SMITH, D. 1875

IRISH.

New-chwang.

CARSON, J. 1874
Hunter, J., M.D. 1869

SCOTCH U.P.

Che-foo.

WESTWATER, A. 1882
Westwater, A. McD., M.D. 1881

New-chwang.

ROSS, JOHN 1872
WEBSTER, J. 1882
CHRISTIE, —, M.D. 1882

Absent.

WILLIAMSON, A., LL.D. 1855
MACINTYRE, M. 1872

CANADIAN.

Tam-sui.

MACKAY, G., D.D. 1871
JAMIESON, R. 1884

SCOTCH ESTABLISHED.

I-chang.

COCKBURN, G. 1878
DOWSLEY, A. 1880

Absent.

WOOD, P. 1878

Methodist Missions, 1851.

WESLEYAN.

Wu-ch'ang.

HILL, DAVID* 1865
TOMLINSON, W. S. 1875

Han-kow.

SCARBOROUGH, W.* 1865
MITCHELL, C. W.* 1873

Han-yang.

NIGHTINGALE, A. 1874
NORTH, T. E.* 1880

Wu-sueh.

BRAMFITT, T. 1875

Fat-shan.

WENYON, C., M.D. 1880

Canton.

BONE, C.* 1880
MARRIS, G.* 1880

Shiu-kwan.

SELBY, T. G.* 1868
HARGREAVES, G. 1878

Absent.

PARKES, H. 1864
BREWER, J. W. 1872
MASTERS, F. J. 1874
FORDHAM, J. S. 1878

NEW CONNECTION.

Tien-tsin.

INNOCENT, J. 1860
CANDLIN, G. T. 1878

Wu-ting.

ROBINSON, J. 1877
HINDS, J. 1879
Stenhouse, D., L.R.C.P., &c. 1878

FREE CHURCH.

Ning-po.

GALPIN, F. 1868
SWALLOW, R. 1874
Croft, Miss 1881

Hang-chau.

SOOTHILL, W. E. 1882

Various.

CHINA INLAND MISSION.

T'ai-yüen.

PIGOTT, T. W. 1879
LANGMAN, A.* 1884
KING, T.* 1884
KEY, W.* 1884
Edwards, E. H., M.B., C.M.* 1882
Horne, Miss 1876
Lancaster, Miss 1880

P'ing-yang.

DRAKE, S. B. 1878
RENDALL, GEORGE 1883
Kingsbury, Miss 1880

Che-foo.

BALLER, F. W. 1873
DOUTHWAITE, A. 1874
ELLISTON, W. L. 1878
Pruen, W. L., L.R.C.P.* 1880
Sharland, Mrs. 1880
Pruen, Mrs. 1882
Cheney, Mrs. 1883
Whitchurch, Miss 1883

Yang-chau.

PARROTT, A. G. 1878
STURMAN, J. H.* 1883
BURNETT, W. E.* 1883

Shang-hai.

JUDD, C. H. 1868
DALZIEL, J. 1878
Seed, Miss 1883
Minchin, Miss 1883
Fowles, Miss 1883

Shao-hing.

MEADOWS, J. 1862
Murray, Miss 1876

Fung-hwa.

WILLIAMSON, J. 1866

T'ai-chau.

RUDLAND, W. D. 1866

Wen-chow.

STOTT, GEORGE 1866
JACKSON, J. A.* 1866
WHILLER, A. 1878

Kiu-chau.

RANDLE, H. 1876
Boyd, Miss 1878
Carpenter, Miss S. 1883
Carpenter, Miss M. 1883

Gan-k'ing.

TOMALIN, E. 1879
COOPER, W.* 1881
WOOD, F. M.* 1883
Hughes, Miss 1876
Evans, Miss Mary 1883
Williams, Miss L. C. 1883
Malpas, Miss 1883

Ta-ku-t'ang.

CARDWELL, J. E. 1868

Wu-ch'ang.

COULTHARD, J. J.* 1879
TAYLOR, H. H.* 1881
DICK, H.* 1883

Ho-nan.†

SAMBROOK, A. W.* 1879

Han-chung.

EASTON, G. F. 1875
PEARSE, E. 1876
Wilson, Miss 1876
Goodman, Miss 1883
Muir, Miss 1883
Black, Miss J. 1883
Black, Miss H. 1883
Black, Miss E. 1883

Si-gan.

KING, GEORGE* 1875
Wilson, Wm., M.B., C.M.* 1882

Ts'in-chau.

PARKER, GEORGE 1876
HUNT, H. W. 1879
Jones, Miss H. 1881

Chung-k'ing.

NICOLL, G. 1875
Fausset, Miss 1878

Chen-tu.

RILEY, J. H. 1878
CLARKE, SAM. R.* 1878
THOMPSON, D.* 1881
Stroud, Miss 1882
Dowman, Miss 1883
Butland, Miss 1883

Kwei-yang.

BROUMTON, J. F. 1875
WINDSOR, THOS.* 1884
HUGHESDEN, E.* 1884

Yün-nan Fu.

EASON, A. E. 1881

Ta-li Fu.

CLARKE, GEO. W.* 1875
ANDREW, GEO. 1881
STEVENS, F. A.* 1883
STEVENSON, O.* 1883

Hu-nan‡.

DORWARD, A. C.* 1878

Bhamô.

SOLTAU, H. 1875

Absent.

TAYLOR, J. HUDSON 1854
STEVENSON, J. W. 1866
MCCARTHY, J. 1868
CAMERON, J.* 1875
LANDALE, R. J.* 1876
MOORE, C. G. 1878
TRENCH, F.* 1878
Turner, Miss 1872
Kerr, Miss 1880

BAPTIST MISSIONARY SOCIETY.

T'ai-yüen.

RICHARD, T. 1869
SOWERBY, A. 1881

† Head-quarters, Fan-ch'eng, HU-PEH.
‡ Head-quarters, Sha-shï, HU-PEH.

Ts'in -chau.

KITTS, J. T. 1879
WHITEWRIGHT, J. S. 1881
JAMES, F. 1876

Absent.

JONES, A. G. 1877
TURNER, J. J. 1876

FEMALE EDUCATION SOCIETY.

Ning-po.

Smith, Miss 1880

Hong-kong.

Johnstone, Miss 1874

UNCONNECTED.

Han-kow.

FOSTER, A. 1871

Hong-kong.

FABER, E. 1865

Hai-nan.

JEREMIASSEN, C. 1882

Che-foo.

Downing, Miss 1866

T'ai-yüen.

Kemb, Miss S. F. 1882

AMERICAN SOCIETIES.

Congregational, 1830.

AM. BOARD C.F.M.

Kalgan.

WILLIAMS, M. 1866
SPRAGUE, W. P. 1874
ROBERTS, J. H. 1877
CHAPIN, F. M. 1880
MURDOCH, MISS, M.D. 1881
Diament, Miss 1870
Garretson, Miss 1880

Pe-kin.

BLODGET, H., D.D. 1854
AMENT, W. S. 1877
NOBLE, W. C. 1878
Chapin, Miss 1874
Haven, Miss 1879

T'ung-chau.

GOODRICH, C. 1865
SHEFFIELD, D. Z. 1869
HOLBROOK, MISS, M.D. 1881
Andrews, Miss 1868

Tien-tsin.

STANLEY, C. A. 1862
PERKINS, H. P. 1881

T'ai-yüen.

STIMSON, M. L. 1881
CADY, C. M.* 1882
ATWOOD, I. J. 1882
TENNY, C. D. 1882
PRICE, J. 1883

Pao-ting.

PIERSON, I.* 1870
Peck, A. P., M.D. 1880
Pierson, Miss 1877
Hale, Miss 1883

P'ang-chia.

SMITH, A. H. 1872
PORTER, H. D., M.D. 1872
Porter, Miss 1868

Foo-chow.

BALDWIN, C., D.D. 1848
HARTWELL, C.* 1853
Newton, Miss 1878
Hartwell, Miss 1884

Shao-wu.

WALKER, J. E. 1874

Hong-kong.

HAGER, C. R. 1883

Absent.

WOODIN, S. F. 1860
CHAPIN, L. D. 1863
Whitney H. T., M.D. 1877
Evans, Miss Jennie 1872

Baptist, 1834.

BAPTIST MISSIONARY UNION.

Ning-po.

LORD, E. C., D.D.* 1848
GODDARD, J. R. 1868
MASON, G. L. 1880
Barchet, S. P., M.D. 1868
Lightfoot, Miss 1879
Inveen, Miss 1879

Shao-hing.

JENKINS, H. 1860

Kin-hwa.

ADAMS, J. 1875

Swa-tow.

ASHMORE, W., D.D. 1851
PARTRIDGE, S. B.* 1868
McKIBBEN, W. K. 1875
ASHMORE, W., Jun. 1880
DANIELS, MISS, M.D. 1878
Thompson, Miss 1876
Norwood, Miss 1877

Absent.

Fielde, Miss 1866

BAPTIST, SOUTHERN.

Teng-chau.

CRAWFORD, T. P., D.D. 1852
HOLCOMB, N. W.* 1881
PRUITT, C. W. 1882
Moon, Miss 1878
Roberts, Miss 1884

Shang-hai.

YATES, M. T., D.D. 1847

Chin-kiang.

HUNNEX, W. J. 1882

Canton.

SIMMONS, E. Z. 1871
GRAVES, R. H., M.D., D.D. 1856
Stein, Miss 1880
Young, Miss 1884

Absent.

Holmes, Mrs. 1859
Whilden, Miss 1872

BAPTIST, SEVENTH DAY.

Shang-hai.

DAVIS, D. H. 1879
SWINNEY, MISS, M.D. 1883

Church Mission, 1835.

PROT. EPISC. MISSION.

Shang-hai.

THOMSON, E. H. 1859
BOONE, W. J. 1869
SAYRES, W. S. 1878
APPLETON, G. H. 1883
Boone, H. W., M.D. 1880
Bruce, Miss 1882
Lawson, Miss 1883
Spencer, Miss 1883

Wu-ch'ang.

GRAVES, F. R. 1881
SOWERBY, H. 1882
LOCK, A. F. 1883
Deas, W. A., M.D.* 1881
Sayres, Mrs. 1883

Methodist Missions, 1847.

METH. EPISC., NORTH.

Pe-kin.

DAVIS, G. R. 1870
PYKE, J. H. 1873
LOWRY, H. H. 1876
GAMEWELL, F. D. 1881
HOBART, W. T. 1882
Cushman, Miss 1878
Sears, Miss 1880
Yates, Miss E. U. 1880
Jewell, Mrs. 1883

Tien-tsin.

WALKER, W. F. 1870
PILCHER, L. W. 1873
HOWARD, MISS, M.D. 1877
AKERS, MISS, M.D. 1882

Chung-k'ing.

WHEELER, L. N., D.D. 1866
LEWIS, S. 1881
Crews, —, M.D. 1883
Wheeler, Miss 1881

Kiu-kiang.

HART, V. C. 1866
HYKES, J. R. 1873
KUPFER, C. F. 1882
WORLEY, H. 1882

Wu-hu.

WOODALL, G. W. 1882

Chin-kiang.

TAFT, M. L. 1880
WORLEY, T. H. 1882
LONGDEN, R. 1883

Foo-chow.

OHLINGER, F. 1870
PLUMB, N. J. 1870
SMYTH, G. B. 1882
WILCOX, M. C.* 1882
TRASK, MISS, M.D. 1874

Absent.

BALDWIN, S., D.D. 1859
SITES, N. 1861
CHANDLER, D. W. 1874
WILLITS, O. W. 1880
SPARR, MISS, M.D. 1878

METH. EPISC., SOUTH.

Shang-hai.

LAMBUTH, J.W., D.D. 1855
ALLEN, Y. J., LL.D. 1860
ROYALL, W. W. 1880
LOEHR, G. R.* 1880
Allen, Miss M. 1878
Muse, Miss 1882

Su-chau.

PARKER, A. P. 1875
REID, C. F. 1879
ANDERSON, D. L. 1882
LAMBUTH, W. R., M.D. 1878
Park, W. H., M.D.* 1882

Nan-siang.

MINGLEDORF, O. G. 1882
Rankin, Miss L. 1878
Rankin, Miss D. 1879

Presbyterian Missions, 1838.

NORTH.

Pe-kin.

WHERRY, J. 1864
McCOY, D. C. 1869
WHITING, J. L. 1869
LOWRIE, J. W.* 1883
Atterbury, B. C., M.D.* 1879
Strong, Miss 1882
Lowrie, Miss 1883

Tsi-nan.

MURRAY, J. 1876
HUNTER, S. A. D., M.D. 1877

Teng-chau.

MILLS, C. R., D.D.* 1859
MATEER, C. W., D.D. 1863
HAYES, W. M. 1881
Neal, J. B., M.D. 1883
Shaw, Mrs. 1874

Wei-hien.

MATEER, R. 1881
LAUGHLIN, J. H. 1881
Matthewson, J.H., M.D.* 1883

Che-foo.

NEVIUS, J. L., D.D. 1854
CORBETT, H. 1863
LEYENBERGER, J. 1866
REID, G.* 1882
Berry, Miss 1883

Nan-kin.

LEAMAN, C. 1874
ABBEY, R. E. 1882
CHAPIN, O. H. 1882
Allen, H. N., M.D. 1882

Su-chau.

FITCH, G. F. 1870
HAYES, J. N. 1882

Shang-hai.

HOLT, W. S. 1873
SMITH, J. N. B.* 1881

Ning-po.

BUTLER, J. 1868
McKEE, W. J. 1879
Warner, Miss 1878

Hang-chau.

JUDSON, J. H. 1879
MILLS, F. V. 1883

Canton.

HAPPER, A., D.D. 1844
NOYES, H. V. 1866
FULTON, A. A. 1880
WHITE, W. J. 1880
Kerr, J. G., M.D. 1854
THOMSON, J., M.D. 1881
NILES, MISS, M.D. 1882
Noyes, Miss H. 1868
Happer, Miss M. 1879
Happer, Miss A. 1880
Butler, Miss 1881

Absent.

FARNHAM, J., D.D. 1860
HENRY, B. C. 1873
Smith, H. R., M.D. 1881
KELSEY, MISS, M.D. 1878
Douw, Miss 1869
Noyes, Miss M. 1873
Anderson, Miss 1878

SOUTH.

Hang-chau.

STUART, J. L. 1868
SYDENSTRICKER, A. 1880
JOHNSON, J. F.* 1883
Randolph, Mrs. 1872
Kirkland, Miss 1875

Su-chau.

DU BOSE, H. C. 1872
DAVIS, J. W. 1873
Stafford, Miss 1873

Chin-kiang.

WOODBRIDGE, S. J.* 1882
WOODS, H. M. 1884

Absent.

PAINTER, G. W.* 1878

REFORMED DUTCH.

Amoy.

TALMAGE, J., D.D. 1847
RAPALJE, D. 1859
KIP, L. W., D.D. 1861
VANDYKE, A. S. 1884
Talmage, Miss M. 1873
Talmage, Miss C. 1883

Various.

WOMEN'S UNION MISSION.

Shang-hai.

REIFSNYDER, MISS, M.D. 1883
Burnett, Miss 1875
Pruyn, Mrs. 1883

BIBLE SOCIETY, AMERICAN.

Shang-hai.

GULICK, L. H., LL.D. 1876
WILLS, W. A. 1876
WARE, J. 1881

Chin-kiang.

COPP, A. 1878
PROTHEROE, T.* 1881

Pe-kin.

BAGNALL, B.* 1871

Hong-kong.

TAYLOR, J.* 1883

Foo-chow.

AMINOFF, J.* 1884

CONTINENTAL MISSIONS.

BASLE MISSION.

Hong-kong.

LECHLER, R. 1847
REUSCH, G. 1872

Chong-lok.

BENDER, H. 1862
ZIEGLER, H. 1871
SCHAIBLE, D. 1877

Sin-on.

MORGENROTH, G. 1877
KAMMERER, P. 1877
SCHULZE, O.* 1881

Li-long.

PITON, C. P. 1864
LOERCHER, J. G. 1865
SCHAUB, M. 1874

Yun-on.

OTT, R. 1878
LEONHARDT, J.* 1881

Absent.

GAUSSMANN, G. 1869

BERLIN MISSION.

Canton.

HUBRIG, F. 1866
TENTSCH, F. 1882
REINHARDT, C. 1882
LEHMANN, T. 1883
Süss, Miss 1862
Brandt, Miss 1864
Schroeder, Miss 1873
Schnaebeli, Miss 1883

BERLIN FOUNDLING HOSPITAL.

Hong-kong.

HARTMAN, F. 1883

RHENISH MISSION.

Canton.

DIETRICH, W. 1877
GERIAHR, J. 1883

APPENDIX B.

STATISTICAL SUMMARY OF PROTESTANT MISSIONS IN CHINA,

DECEMBER 31ST, 1886.—*From "The Chinese Recorder" (corrected).*

	NAME OF SOCIETY.	Date of Mission.	Foreign Missionaries.				Native Ordained Ministers.	Un-ordained Native Helpers.	Adult Communicants.	Pupils in Schools.	Contributions by Native Churches.
			Men.	Wives.	Single Women.	Total.					$
1	London Missionary Society	1807	24	17	6	47	8	66	3,052	1,711	...
2	A. B. C. F. M.	1830	26	25	12	63	...	80	1,175	...	...
3	American Baptist, North	1834	9	9	5	23	8	72	1,433	175	491·26
4	American Protestant Episcopal	1835	11	9	3	23	17	13	384	801	500·80
5	American Presbyterian, North	1838	44	32	14	90	14	16	4,368	1,804	1,472·00
6	British and Foreign Bible Society	1843	11	5	...	16	...	82	...	...	...
7	Church Missionary Society	1844	24	23	...	47	4	186	2,724	1,089	2,103·00
8	English Baptist*	1845	15	14	1	30	...	17	994	46	...
9	Methodist Episcopal, North	1847	24	24	12	60	68(?)	136	2,408	988	3,121·10
10	Seventh Day Baptist	1847	1	1	1	3	...	8	18	69	88·00
11	American Baptist, South	1847	11	9	4	24	...	...	547	...	600·00
12	Basel Mission	1847	19	19	...	38	4	49	1,611	461	...
13	English Presbyterian	1847	22	17	7	46	5	121	3,312	...	1,524·74 †
14	Rhenish Mission	1847	3	3	...	6	...	6	60	200	...
15	Methodist Episcopal, South	1848	8	8	7	23	3	7	146	653	222·11
16	Berlin Foundling Hospital	1850	1	1	4	6	...	...	...	80	...
17	Wesleyan Missionary Society	1852	20	8	4	32	...	28	679	587	...
18	American Reformed (Dutch)	1858	5	5	2	12	3(?)	20	784	...	2,008·43
19	Women's Union Mission	1859	...	...	3	3	...	...	...	...	...
20	Methodist New Connection*	1860	6	5	...	11	...	54	1,186	142	...
21	Society for Promotion of Female Education	1864	...	...	3	3	...	...	...	...	...
22	United Presbyterian, Scotland	1865	7	6	...	13	...	17	306	...	...
23	China Inland Mission	1865	92	41	55	188	12	102	1,314	274	408·13
24	National Bible Society, Scotland	1868	3	2	...	5	...	40(?)	...	...	...
25	United Methodist Free Church	1868	3	3	...	6	...	10	297	...	300·00
26	American Presbyterian, South	1868	8	6	4	18	...	10	44	207	35·00
27	Irish Presbyterian	1869	3	3	...	6	...	...	...	...	...
28	Canadian Presbyterian*	1871	2	2	...	4	...	32	1,128	55	...
29	Society for Propagation of the Gospel	1874	4	2	...	6	...	...	...	...	...
30	American Bible Society	1876	8	4	...	12	...	40	...	...	...
31	Established Church, Scotland	1878	2	2	...	4	...	3	30	438	...
32	Berlin Mission*	1882	5	5	...	10	...	27	119	84	...
33	General Protestant Evang. Society	1884	2	...	...	2	...	...	...	...	...
34	Bible Christians	1885	2	...	...	2	...	...	...	...	...
35	Disciples of Christ	1886	3	...	...	3	...	...	...	...	...
36	Book and Tract Society	1886	1	...	...	1	...	...	...	...	...
37	Independent Workers	...	3	...	2	5	...	...	...	...	...
	TOTAL	...	432	310	149	891	146	1,242	28,119	9,864	$12,874·57

CPSIA information can be obtained
at www.ICGtesting.com
Printed in the USA
LVHW061924160119
604162LV00008B/220/P

9 781108 014519